STECK-VAUGHN

Level F

LANGUAGE Exercises

TEACHER'S GUIDE

STECK-VAUGHN®
COMPANY
ELEMENTARY • SECONDARY • ADULT • LIBRARY

Table of Contents

Acknowledgments

Executive Editor: Diane Sharpe
Supervising Editor: Stephanie Muller
Project Editor: Patricia Claney
Design Manager: Laura Cole

LANGUAGE EXERCISES Series:

Level A	Level D	Level G
Level B	Level E	Level H
Level C	Level F	Review

ISBN 0-8114-6319-2

3 4 5 6 7 8 9 RP 00 99

Introduction

Language Exercises is a program designed for students who require additional practice in the basics of effective writing and speaking. Focused practice in key grammar, usage, mechanics, and composition areas helps students gain ownership of essential skills. The logical sequence of the practice exercises, combined with a clear and concise format, allows for easy and independent use.

Focus on Key Skills

Language Exercises provides systematic, focused attention to just one carefully selected skill at a time. Rules are clearly stated at the beginning of each lesson. Key terms are introduced in bold type. The rules are then illustrated with examples and followed by meaningful practice exercises.

Lessons are organized around a series of units. They are arranged in a logical sequence beginning with vocabulary, progressing through sentences, grammar and usage, mechanics, and culminating with composition skills.

Levels C through H and Review include a final unit on study skills, which can be assigned as needed. This unit includes such skills as organizing information, following directions, using a dictionary, using the library, and choosing appropriate reference sources.

Skills are reviewed thoroughly in a two-page Review at the conclusion of each unit and in the twelve-page Final Review at the end of the book. Also, the last twelve pages of this Teacher's Guide provide six two-page blackline master Unit Tests presented in a standardized test format. The content of each unit is repeated and expanded in subsequent levels as highlighted in the Scope and Sequence chart on the next two pages.

Application Is the Key

Throughout the program, *Language Exercises* stresses the application of language principles. In addition to matching, circling, or underlining elements in a predetermined sentence, lessons ask students to use what they have learned in an original sentence or in rewriting a sentence. *Using What You've Learned,* a two-page lesson at the end of each unit, provides students with an opportunity to "pull together" what they have learned in the unit and apply their learning to a writing situation.

Easy-to-Use Lessons

From the beginning, students feel comfortable with the format of the lessons. Each lesson is introduced with a rule at the top of the page and ends with a meaningful exercise at the bottom of the page. Each lesson is clearly labeled, and directions are clear and uncomplicated. Because the format is logical and consistent and the vocabulary is carefully controlled, most students can use *Language Exercises* with a high degree of independence. As the teacher, this allows you the time needed to help students on a one-to-one basis.

Attention to Composition Skills

The process approach to teaching writing provides success for most students. *Language Exercises* provides direct support for the teaching of composition and significantly enhances those strategies and techniques commonly associated with the process-writing approach.

Each book includes a composition unit that provides substantial work with important composition skills, such as writing topic sentences, selecting supporting details, taking notes, writing reports, and revising and proofreading. Also included in the composition unit is practice with various prewriting activities, such as clustering and brainstorming, which play an important role in process writing. The composition lessons are presented in the same rule-plus-practice format as in other units.

Teacher's Guide

The Teacher's Guide for each level of *Language Exercises* includes a two-page Scope and Sequence chart and an Answer Key in an easy-to-use format for all exercises.

The final section of the Teacher's Guide includes six two-page blackline master Unit Tests presented in a standardized test format. The skills and concepts included on these tests parallel the skills in the end-of-unit Reviews in the student book. These Unit Tests can also be used as both pre- and post-tests. Answers for these tests appear at the end of the Answer Key.

SCOPE AND SEQUENCE

	A	B	C	D	E	F	G	H	Review
Vocabulary									
Sound Words (Onomatopoeia)	■								
Rhyming Words	■	■							
Synonyms	■	■	■	■	■	■	■	■	■
Antonyms	■	■	■	■	■	■	■	■	■
Homonyms	■	■	■	■	■	■	■	■	■
Multiple Meanings/Homographs	■	■	■	■	■	■	■	■	■
Prefixes and Suffixes			■	■	■	■	■	■	■
Base and Root Words			■	■	■	■	■	■	■
Compound Words			■	■	■	■	■	■	■
Contractions			■	■	■	■	■	■	■
Idioms						■	■	■	■
Connotation/Denotation						■	■	■	■
Sentences									
Word Order in Sentences	■	■							
Recognizing a Sentence	■	■	■	■	■	■	■	■	■
Subjects and Predicates	■	■	■	■	■	■	■	■	■
Types of Sentences	■	■	■	■	■	■	■	■	■
Compound/Complex Sentences			■	■	■	■	■	■	■
Sentence Combining			■	■	■	■	■	■	■
Run-On Sentences				■	■	■	■	■	■
Independent and Subordinate Clauses							■	■	■
Compound Subjects and Predicates						■	■	■	■
Direct and Indirect Objects							■	■	■
Inverted Word Order						■	■	■	■
Grammar and Usage									
Common and Proper Nouns	■	■	■	■	■	■	■	■	■
Singular and Plural Nouns	■	■	■	■	■	■	■	■	■
Possessive Nouns				■	■	■	■	■	■
Appositives						■	■	■	■
Verbs	■	■	■	■	■	■	■	■	■
Verb Tense	■	■	■	■	■	■	■	■	■
Regular/Irregular Verbs	■	■	■	■	■	■	■	■	■
Subject/Verb Agreement		■	■	■	■	■	■	■	■
Verb Phrases						■	■	■	■
Transitive and Intransitive Verbs							■	■	■
Verbals: Gerunds, Participles, and Infinitives							■	■	■
Active and Passive Voice							■	■	■
Mood								■	■
Pronouns	■	■	■	■	■	■	■	■	■
Antecedents							■	■	■
Articles	■	■	■						
Adjectives	■	■	■	■	■	■	■	■	■
Correct Word Usage (e.g. *may/can, sit/set*)	■	■	■	■	■	■	■	■	■
Adverbs			■	■	■	■	■	■	■
Prepositions					■	■	■	■	■
Prepositional Phrases						■	■	■	■
Conjunctions						■	■	■	■
Interjections						■	■	■	
Double Negatives								■	■
Capitalization and Punctuation									
Capitalization: First Word in Sentence	■	■	■	■	■	■	■		■
Capitalization: Proper Nouns	■	■	■	■	■	■	■	■	■
Capitalization: in Letters		■	■	■	■	■	■	■	■
Capitalization: Abbreviations		■	■	■	■	■	■	■	■
Capitalization: Titles		■	■	■	■	■	■	■	■

	A	B	C	D	E	F	G	H	Review
Capitalization and Punctuation (cont'd)									
Capitalization: Proper Adjectives					■	■	■	■	■
End Punctuation	■	■	■	■	■	■	■	■	■
Commas		■	■	■	■	■	■	■	■
Apostrophes in Contractions		■	■	■	■	■	■	■	■
Apostrophes in Possessives			■	■	■	■	■	■	■
Quotation Marks			■	■	■	■	■	■	■
Colons/Semicolons						■	■	■	■
Hyphens						■	■	■	■
Composition									
Expanding Sentences					■	■	■	■	■
Writing a Paragraph		■	■	■	■	■	■	■	■
Paragraphs: Topic Sentence (main idea)		■	■	■	■	■	■	■	■
Paragraphs: Supporting Details		■	■	■	■	■	■	■	■
Order In Paragraphs		■	■	■	■	■	■		■
Writing Process:									
Establishing Purpose			■	■		■	■	■	■
Audience					■	■	■	■	■
Topic			■	■	■	■	■	■	■
Outlining				■		■	■	■	■
Clustering/Brainstorming					■		■	■	■
Notetaking						■	■		
Revising/Proofreading					■	■	■	■	■
Types of Writing:									
Poem	■								
Letter	■	■	■			■			
"How-to" Paragraph			■						
Invitation			■						
Telephone Message			■						
Conversation				■					
Narrative Paragraph				■					
Comparing and Contrasting					■				
Descriptive Paragraph					■				
Report						■			
Interview							■		
Persuasive Composition								■	■
Readiness/Study Skills									
Grouping	■								
Letters of Alphabet	■								
Listening	■	■							
Making Comparisons	■	■							
Organizing Information	■	■	■						
Following Directions	■	■	■	■	■				
Alphabetical Order	■	■	■	■	■	■	■	■	■
Using a Dictionary:									
Definitions		■	■	■	■	■	■	■	■
Guide Words/Entry Words		■	■	■	■	■	■	■	■
Syllables			■	■	■	■	■	■	■
Pronunciation			■	■	■	■	■	■	■
Multiple Meanings				■	■	■	■	■	■
Word Origins						■	■	■	■
Parts of a Book			■	■	■	■	■	■	■
Using the Library						■	■	■	■
Using Encyclopedias				■	■	■	■	■	■
Using Reference Books						■	■	■	■
Using the *Readers' Guide*							■	■	■
Using Tables, Charts, Graphs, and Diagrams						■	■	■	■
Choosing Appropriate Sources						■	■	■	■

Answer Key

Unit 1 Vocabulary

Lesson 1, Synonyms and Antonyms (P. 1)

A. Synonyms will vary.

B. **1.** begin **2.** fall **3.** sick **4.** tired **5.** close

C. Antonyms will vary.

D. **1.** heavy **2.** late **3.** kind **4.** empty **5.** found

Lesson 2, Homonyms (P. 2)

A.
1. beach
2. deer
3. weigh
4. pane
5. to, to, two
6. knew, new
7. their
8. ate, eight
9. sea
10. Ring
11. here
12. write, right
13. read
14. buy, by
15. tale

B.
1. haul
2. through
3. week
4. they're or their
5. herd
6. hear
7. buy or bye
8. pain
9. heel or he'll
10. blue
11. flour
12. stare
13. pail
14. wring
15. sore
16. sail
17. one
18. I'll or isle
19. road or rowed
20. meat or mete
21. hour
22. see
23. write or rite
24. piece
25. know
26. great
27. weigh or whey
28. sent or scent
29. do or due
30. fourth

Lesson 3, Homographs (P. 3)

A. **1.** checks **2.** interest **3.** vault **4.** interest **5.** vault **6.** checks

B. Sentences will vary.

1. a **2.** a **3.** a **4.** a **5.** b

Lesson 4, Prefixes (P. 4)

A. Definitions will vary.

1. impractical
2. misbehave
3. uneasy
4. nonviolent
5. unusual

B. Meanings will vary.

1. un-
2. dis-
3. dis-
4. mis-
5. pre-
6. re-
7. mis-
8. im-
9. non-
10. un-
11. in-
12. pre-

Lesson 5, Suffixes (P. 5)

A. Definitions will vary.

1. mountainous
2. helpful
3. snowy
4. national
5. knowledgeable

B. Meanings will vary.

1. -able
2. -less
3. -ous
4. -able
5. -ous
6. -able
7. -ous
8. -ful
9. -y
10. -less
11. -al
12. -al

Lesson 6, Contractions (P. 6)

A.
1. they're, they are
2. won't, will not
3. There's, There is
4. That's, That is; shouldn't, should not
5. weren't, were not
6. doesn't, does not
7. can't, cannot; it's, it is
8. they've, they have; they'll, they will
9. It's, It is; aren't, are not
10. they'd, they would

B.
1. I have, I've; I would, I'd
2. It is, It's; what is, what's
3. I will, I'll
4. does not, doesn't

Lesson 7, Compound Words (P. 7)

A. Answers will vary.

B. **1.** forehead
2. haircut
3. everywhere
4. newsstand
5. loudspeaker
6. everything

Lesson 8, Connotation/Denotation (P. 8)

A. **1.** wonderful
2. Brave
3. fascinating
4. hilarious
5. smile

B. **1.** cheap **4.** silly
2. soggy **5.** smirk
3. nagged **6.** frightened

C. **1.** antique **5.** disaster
2. slender **6.** sip
3. thrifty **7.** starving
4. parade **8.** filthy

Lesson 9, Idioms (P. 9)

A. **1.** j **6.** f
2. i **7.** d
3. h **8.** g
4. a **9.** b
5. e **10.** c

B. Meanings will vary.
1. in hot water
2. beside themselves
3. fly off the handle
4. shaken up
5. talk turkey

Review (P. 10)

A. Synonyms and antonyms will vary.

B. **1.** plane, there
2. week, to, see
3. bear, would
4. cheap, break, week

C. Sentences will vary.
1. a **3.** a
2. b **4.** b

D. Meanings will vary.
1. im-, not possible **5.** dis-, not interested
2. in-, not complete **6.** re-, furnish again
3. un-, not easy **7.** mis-, pronounce incorrectly
4. non-, not violent **8.** pre-, before history

Review (P. 11)

E. **1.** -ous, full of hazards
2. -less, without help
3. -able, to be able to profit
4. -al, relating to a region

F. **1.** we'll **4.** they've
2. she'd **5.** you'll
3. won't **6.** we're

G. **1.** crossroad
2. sandlot
3. snowplow
4. tabletop

H. **1.** inexpensive **3.** curious
2. cozy **4.** relaxed

I. Meanings will vary.
1. stay on your toes
2. run across
3. saw red
4. all ears

Using What You've Learned (P. 12)

A. Sentences will vary.

B. Sentences will vary.

C. Sentences will vary.
1. knew
2. greater
3. chews
4. wait
5. waste

D. Sentences will vary.

Using What You've Learned (P. 13)

E. Words will vary.

F. Sentences will vary.

G. Words will vary. Suggested:
1. soggy; moist
2. holler; call
3. skinny; slender
4. ancient; elderly
5. gab, discuss
6. rags, apparel
7. beg; request
8. chore; job
9. hack; carve
10. devour; dine

Unit 2 Sentences

Lesson 10, Recognizing Sentences (P. 14)

S should precede the following sentences, and students should end each with a period: 2, 5, 7, 9, 10, 11, 12, 13, 16, 19, 20, 21, 22, 24, 28, 29.

Lesson 11, Types of Sentences (P. 15)

1. IN	**8.** D	**15.** IN	**22.** D
2. IN	**9.** IN	**16.** D	**23.** D
3. D	**10.** IN	**17.** D	**24.** IN
4. D	**11.** D	**18.** IN	**25.** D
5. D	**12.** D	**19.** D	**26.** IN
6. IN	**13.** IN	**20.** IN	**27.** IN
7. D	**14.** D	**21.** IN	**28.** D

Lesson 12, More Types of Sentences (P. 16)

1. IM	**8.** IM	**15.** E	**22.** IM
2. IM	**9.** IM	**16.** E	**23.** E
3. E	**10.** IM	**17.** E	**24.** IM
4. IM	**11.** E	**18.** IM	**25.** IM
5. E	**12.** IM	**19.** IM	**26.** IM
6. IM or E	**13.** E	**20.** E	**27.** E
7. IM	**14.** E	**21.** E	**28.** E

Lesson 13, Complete Subjects and Predicates (P. 17)

1. Bees / fly.
2. Trains / whistle.
3. A talented artist / drew . . .
4. The wind / blew . . .
5. My grandmother / made . . .
6. We / surely . . .
7. These cookies / are . . .
8. This letter / came . . .
9. They / rent . . .
10. Jennifer / is . . .
11. Our baseball team / won . . .
12. The band / played . . .
13. A cloudless sky / is . . .
14. The voice of the auctioneer / was . . .
15. A sudden flash of lightning / startled . . .
16. The wind / howled . . .
17. Paul's dog / followed . . .
18. Their apartment / is . . .
19. We / have . . .
20. Each player on the team / deserves . . .
21. Forest rangers / fought . . .
22. A friend / taught . . .
23. Millions of stars / make . . .
24. The airplane / was . . .
25. Many of the children / waded . . .
26. Yellowstone Park / is . . .
27. Cold weather / is . . .
28. The trees / were . . .

Lesson 14, Simple Subjects and Predicates (P. 18)

1. A sudden clap of thunder / frightened . . .
2. The soft snow / covered . . .
3. We / drove . . .
4. The students / are making . . .
5. Our class / read . . .
6. The women / were talking . . .
7. This album / has . . .
8. We / are furnishing . . .
9. All the trees on that lawn / are . . .
10. Many Americans / are working . . .
11. The manager / read . . .
12. Bill / brought . . .
13. We / opened . . .
14. The two mechanics / worked . . .
15. Black and yellow butterflies / fluttered . . .
16. The child / spoke . . .
17. We / found . . .
18. The best part of the program / is . . .
19. Every ambitious person / is working . . .
20. Sheryl / swam . . .
21. Our program / will begin . . .
22. The handle of this basket / is . . .
23. The clock in the tower / strikes . . .
24. The white farmhouse on that road / belongs . . .
25. The first game of the season / will be played . . .

Lesson 15, Subjects and Predicates in Inverted Order (P. 19)

A. Sentences 1, 3, 4, 5, 6, 8, 9, 11, and 12 are in inverted order.

1. Lightly falls / the mist.
2. The peaches on this tree / are ripe now.
3. Over and over rolled / the rocks.
4. Down the street marched / the band.
5. Near the ocean are / many birds.
6. Right under the chair ran / the kitten.
7. He / hit the ball a long way.
8. Along the ridge hiked / the campers.
9. Underground is / the stream.
10. The fish / jumped in the lake.
11. Over the hill came / the trucks.
12. Out came / the rainbow.

B.
1. The mist falls lightly.
2. The rocks rolled over and over.
3. The band marched down the street.
4. Many birds are near the ocean.
5. The kitten ran right under the chair.
6. The campers hiked along the ridge.
7. The stream is underground.
8. The trucks came over the hill.
9. The rainbow came out.

Lesson 16, Using Compound Subjects (P. 20)

A. Sentences 1, 2, 3, 4, 6, 7, 8, and 9 have compound subjects.

1. English settlers and Spanish settlers / came . . .
2. Trees and bushes / were . . .
3. The fierce winds and the cold temperatures / made . . .
4. The settlers and Native Americans / became . . .
5. Native Americans / helped . . .
6. Potatoes and corn / were . . .
7. English settlers and Spanish settlers / had . . .
8. Peanuts and sunflower seeds / are . . .
9. Lima beans and corn / are . . .
10. Zucchini / is . . .
11. Native Americans / also . . .

B.

1. Gold and silver from the New World were sent to Spain.
2. France and the Netherlands staked claims in the Americas in the 1500s and 1600s.
3. John Cabot and Henry Hudson explored areas of the Americas.

C. Sentences will vary.

Lesson 17, Using Compound Predicates (P. 21)

A. Sentences 2, 3, 4, 6, 8, 9, 11, and 12 have compound predicates.

1. The students / organized a picnic for their families.
2. They / discussed and chose a date for the picnic.
3. They / wrote and designed invitations.
4. The invitations / were mailed and delivered promptly.
5. Twenty-five families / responded to the invitations.
6. The students / bought the food and made the sandwiches.
7. The families / bought the soft drinks.
8. The students / packed and loaded the food into a truck.
9. The families / brought and set up the volleyball nets.
10. Everyone / participated in the games and races.
11. They / ran relay races and threw water balloons.
12. Everyone / packed the food and cleaned up the picnic area at the end of the day.

B.

1. Caroline heard and memorized the music.
2. Keith picked up and loaded the newspapers into his car.
3. Larry studied and wrote down the names of the states.

C. Sentences will vary.

Lesson 18, Simple and Compound Sentences (P. 22)

A. Sentences 1, 3, 5, and 6 are simple. Sentences 2 and 4 are compound.

1. The seven continents of the world / are North America, South America, Africa, Europe, Australia, Asia, and Antarctica.
2. Three-fourths of the earth / is covered by water, and most of it / is salty ocean water.
3. The four oceans of the world / are the Pacific, the Atlantic, the Indian, and the Arctic.
4. We / cannot exist without water, but we / cannot drink the salty ocean water.
5. Most of the water we drink / comes from lakes, rivers, and streams.
6. Clean water / is a priceless resource.

B.

1. The Pacific Ocean is the largest ocean in the world, and it covers more area than all the earth's land put together.
2. Bodies of salt water that are smaller than oceans are called seas, gulfs, or bays, and these bodies of water are often encircled by land.
3. Seas, gulfs, and bays are joined to the oceans, and they vary in size and depth.
4. The Mediterranean is one of the earth's largest seas, and it is almost entirely encircled by the southern part of Europe, the northern part of Africa, and the western part of Asia.

Lesson 19, Correcting Run-on Sentences (P. 23)

Sentences may vary.

1. In 1860, the Pony Express started in St. Joseph, Missouri. The route began where the railroads ended.
2. People in the West wanted faster mail service. The mail took six weeks by boat.
3. Mail sent by stagecoach took about 21 days. The Pony Express averaged ten days.
4. The Pony Express used a relay system. Riders and horses were switched at 157 places along the way to Sacramento, California.
5. Because teenagers weighed less than adults, most of the riders were teenagers. The horses could run faster carrying them.
6. Riders had to cross raging rivers. The mountains were another barrier.

Lesson 20, Expanding Sentences (P. 24)

A. Sentences will vary.

B. Sentences will vary.

Review (P. 25)

A.

1. IN, ?	**6.** E, !
2. D, .	**7.** IN, ?
3. IM, .	**8.** X
4. X	**9.** E, !
5. D, .	**10.** IN, ?

B. **1.** You / must guess . . .
2. John / will write . . .
3. His younger sister / has already written . . .
4. His twin brothers / will write . . .
5. Each member of the family / hopes . . .
6. Only one person / can win.

C. **1.** Maria's contest entry form came in the mail.
2. Her contestant prize number went right into the trash.
3. The winning prize number was buried in the city dump.
4. Maria will never know what she did.

Review (P. 26)

D.

1. CP	**5.** CS
2. CS	**6.** C
3. R	**7.** CP
4. C	**8.** R

E. **1.** Jan and Paul listened to the song playing on the radio.
2. They both knew the title of the song and remembered who recorded it.

F. Sentences may vary. Suggested:
1. I enjoy entering recipe contests, but my favorite contests are for dessert recipes.
2. I create most of my recipes from scratch, or I add unusual ingredients to existing recipes.

G. Sentences may vary. Suggested:
1. Many people win contests every day. Some people just have to write their names on an entry form to win.
2. Some contest winners are given numbers, and the winning prize numbers are drawn randomly.

H. Sentences will vary.

Using What You've Learned (P. 27)

A. Sentences will vary.
B. Sentences will vary.
C. Sentences will vary.
D. Sentences will vary.

Using What You've Learned (P. 28)

E. Sentences will vary. Suggested:
1. To take a good photograph, you need a good eye. You do not need an expensive camera.
2. You just load your camera and go for a walk.
3. You may see something that is different and colorful.
4. Perhaps you like the shape of an object, or maybe you like the texture.
5. Don't take your picture yet! Be sure your lens cap is off and your camera is focused correctly.
6. Think about what you do not want in your picture and the way you want to frame your picture.
7. Take your time, and keep your camera steady.

F. Sentences will vary.

Unit 3 Grammar and Usage

Lesson 21, Nouns (P. 29)

A. Answers will vary.

B. **1.** Alaska; gold; silver; copper; oil
2. Chocolate; beans; tree; tropics
3. distance; Texas; distance; Chicago; New York
4. men; women; horses; parade
5. city; California; San Diego
6. Alexander Graham Bell; inventor; telephone; Edinburgh, Scotland
7. Jack, Diane, plane; London; Buckingham Palace
8. animals; piranhas; alligators; anacondas; sloths; Amazon River Basin
9. tarantula; type; spider
10. Maya; people; Mexico; Central America

Lesson 22, Common and Proper Nouns (P. 30)

A. Answers will vary.

B. Answers will vary. Suggested:

1. state	**11.** planet
2. continent	**12.** president
3. day	**13.** month
4. river	**14.** mountains
5. person	**15.** country
6. lake	**16.** book
7. holiday	**17.** person
8. ocean	**18.** city
9. state	**19.** city
10. person	**20.** dog

Lesson 22, Common and Proper Nouns (P. 31)

C. **1.** timber; oak; furniture; bridges; ships
2. painter; jeweler; farmer; engineer; inventor
3. crops; sugar; tobacco; coffee; fruits
4. groves; nuts; part

5. rivers; beaches
6. bridge; world
7. foods; lamb; fish; olives; cheese
8. road; tunnel; base; tree
9. civilizations; gold; ornaments
10. lakes
11. tree; blossoms; fruits
12. center
13. trees; turpentine; tar; resin; timber; oils
14. amount; coffee
15. pelican; penguin; flamingo; birds
16. trip; space; danger

D. 1. Brazil
2. William Penn; Pennsylvania
3. Elm Grove Library
4. Commander Byrd; North Pole
5. Dr. Jeanne Spurlock; Howard University College of Medicine
6. Europe; Asia
7. Colombia
8. Kilimanjaro; Africa
9. Navajo
10. Leticia; Carlos; Sam; Ted
11. Thomas Jefferson; United States
12. Lake Michigan
13. Quebec; North America
14. Paul Revere
15. India
16. Sears Tower; Chicago

Lesson 23, Singular and Plural Nouns (P. 32)

A. 1. newspapers
2. guesses
3. towns
4. valleys
5. bodies
6. stories
7. bushes
8. offices
9. taxes
10. toys
11. bosses
12. schools
13. days
14. copies
15. authors
16. porches

B. 1. pennies
2. dresses
3. bridges
4. brushes
5. counties
6. foxes
7. books
8. lunches
9. countries

Lesson 23, Singular and Plural Nouns (P. 33)

C. 1. knives
2. loaves
3. halves
4. mice
5. feet
6. geese
7. hooves
8. moose
9. lives
10. tomatoes
11. teeth
12. pianos

D. 1. feet
2. sheep
3. chimneys
4. cities
5. leaves
6. mosquitoes
7. nickels
8. friends
9. desks
10. benches

Lesson 24, Possessive Nouns (P. 34)

A. 1. girl's
2. child's
3. women's
4. children's
5. John's
6. baby's
7. boys'
8. teacher's
9. Dr. Ray's
10. ladies'
11. brother's
12. soldier's
13. men's
14. aunt's
15. Ms. Jones's

B. 1. Jim's cap
2. Kathy's wrench
3. baby's smile
4. friend's car
5. Kim's new shoes
6. dog's collar
7. Frank's golf clubs
8. runners' shoes
9. parents' friends
10. editor's opinion
11. children's lunches
12. Kyle's coat
13. teacher's assignment

Lesson 24, Possessive Nouns (P. 35)

C. 1. company's
2. dog's
3. women's
4. Doug's
5. David's
6. cat's
7. Kurt's
8. Men's
9. squirrel's
10. brother's
11. child's
12. calf's
13. baby's
14. teachers'
15. Alex's
16. deer's
17. Stacy's
18. country's
19. robins'
20. person's
21. sister's
22. children's
23. neighbors'
24. class's
25. boys'
26. designer's
27. horse's

Lesson 25, Appositives (P. 36)

A. Students should circle the phrases in bold.
1. **my father's older brother**, Henry
2. **the Missouri Pacific**, train
3. **the location of the main station**, Seattle
4. **its main cargo**, Coal and lumber
5. **our uncle**, Henry
6. **his nephews**, us
7. **his brother**, father
8. **his sister-in-law**, mother
9. **his wife**, Aunt Emma
10. **Todd and Elizabeth**, cousins

B. Sentences will vary.

Lesson 26, Verbs (P. 37)

1. are
2. wrote
3. Check
4. have
5. is
6. reached
7. won
8. trains
9. has
10. are
11. remember
12. bought
13. is
14. followed
15. whistled
16. watches
17. scored
18. won
19. is
20. lays
21. set
22. Answer
23. explained
24. worked
25. has
26. plays
27. Brush
28. whirled
29. arrived
30. is

Lesson 27, Verb Phrases (P. 38)

1. were held
2. invented
3. was
4. was
5. built
6. will arrive
7. was
8. has made
9. covered
10. have ridden
11. is molding
12. spent
13. are posted
14. has found
15. is going
16. have trimmed
17. exports
18. is reading
19. helped
20. was discovered
21. was called
22. are planning
23. has howled
24. have arrived
25. have written
26. can name
27. received
28. was printed
29. are working
30. was painted

Lesson 28, Helping Verbs (P. 39)

A. Students should circle the words in bold.

1. **have** begun
2. **will** rake
3. **must** sweep
4. **will** pull
5. **may** prepare
6. **should** wash
7. **would** make
8. **is** working
9. **has** sprayed
10. **must** close
11. **would** enjoy
12. **might** finish

B. Sentences will vary.

Lesson 29, More Helping Verbs (P. 40)

A. Students should circle the words in bold.

1. **will be** given
2. **have been** studying
3. **may be** forming
4. **should be** reviewing
5. **Are** joining
6. **May** meet
7. **should have** known
8. **have** been
9. **have been** looking
10. **would have** met
11. **has been** delayed
12. **Would** prefer
13. **had been** enjoying
14. **have been** waiting
15. **had** been
16. **Will be** swimming
17. **must have been** splashing
18. **Could** take

B. Statements will vary.

C. Questions will vary.

Lesson 30, Using *Is/Are* and *Was/Were* (P. 41)

A.
1. Is
2. are
3. is
4. are
5. is
6. are
7. are
8. Are
9. is
10. are

B.
1. were
2. were
3. were
4. were
5. was
6. was
7. was
8. were
9. were
10. was

Lesson 31, Verb Tenses (P. 42)

A.
1. works; present
2. care; present
3. play; present
4. threw; past
5. sailed; past
6. ran; past
7. shouted; past
8. listens; present
9. got; past
10. called; past
11. went; past
12. will play; future

B.
1. My little sister followed me everywhere.
2. She came to my friend's house.
3. She rode my bicycle on the grass.

Lesson 32, Principal Parts of Verbs (P. 43)

1. is walking; walked; (have, has, had) walked
2. is visiting; visited; (have, has, had) visited
3. is watching; watched; (have, has, had) watched
4. is following; followed; (have, has, had) followed
5. is jumping; jumped; (have, has, had) jumped
6. is talking; talked; (have, has, had) talked
7. is adding; added; (have, has, had) added
8. is learning; learned; (have, has, had) learned
9. is painting; painted; (have, has, had) painted
10. is planting; planted; (have, has, had) planted
11. is working; worked; (have, has, had) worked
12. is dividing; divided; (have, has, had) divided
13. is missing; missed; (have, has, had) missed
14. is scoring; scored; (have, has, had) scored
15. is calling; called; (have, has, had) called
16. is collecting; collected; (have, has, had) collected

Lesson 33, Past Tenses of *See, Do,* and *Come* (P. 44)

1. saw
2. came
3. did
4. saw
5. did
6. came
7. done
8. come
9. seen
10. done
11. came
12. seen
13. come
14. seen
15. came
16. saw
17. did
18. come
19. saw
20. done
21. came
22. did
23. come
24. saw
25. come
26. seen
27. did
28. came
29. saw
30. done

Lesson 34, Past Tenses of *Eat* and *Drink* (P. 45)

A.
1. eaten
2. drank
3. ate
4. drunk
5. ate
6. drank
7. eaten
8. drunk
9. ate
10. drank
11. ate
12. drank
13. eaten
14. drunk
15. eaten
16. drank

B.
1. eaten
2. drank
3. ate
4. drunk
5. drank
6. eaten
7. drank
8. eaten
9. drunk
10. ate

Lesson 35, Past Tenses of *Sing* and *Ring* (P. 46)

A. 1. sung
2. rung
3. sang
4. rung
5. sang
6. rang
7. sang
8. rang
9. sung
10. rang
11. sung
12. rung
13. sang; sung
14. rung
15. sang
16. rung

B. 1. rung
2. sang
3. sung
4. rang
5. rung
6. sang
7. rang
8. sung
9. rang
10. sang

Lesson 36, Past Tenses of *Freeze, Choose, Speak,* and *Break* (P. 47)

A. 1. spoken
2. frozen
3. broke
4. spoken
5. chosen
6. broken
7. spoken
8. froze
9. chose
10. broken
11. spoke
12. froze
13. broken
14. chose
15. spoke
16. frozen

B. 1. frozen
2. broken
3. chosen
4. spoke
5. chosen
6. chose
7. broken
8. spoke
9. frozen
10. spoken

Lesson 37, Past Tenses of *Know, Grow,* and *Throw* (P. 48)

A. 1. known
2. grew
3. thrown
4. known
5. grown
6. thrown
7. grown
8. knew
9. grown
10. known
11. thrown
12. grew
13. threw
14. grown
15. knew
16. threw
17. known
18. grew

B. Sentences will vary.

C. Sentences will vary.

D. Sentences will vary.

Lesson 38, Past Tenses of *Blow* and *Fly* (P. 49)

A. 1. flew
2. blown
3. flown
4. blew
5. blew
6. flown
7. flew
8. blown
9. flew
10. blown
11. flown
12. blown
13. flew
14. blown
15. flown
16. blew
17. flown
18. blew
19. flew
20. blown
21. flew
22. blew
23. flown

B. Sentences will vary.

C. Sentences will vary.

Lesson 39, Past Tenses of *Take* and *Write* (P. 50)

A. 1. took
2. written
3. taken
4. wrote
5. took
6. written
7. took
8. wrote
9. taken
10. written
11. took
12. written
13. took
14. wrote

B. 1. wrote
2. taken
3. written
4. taken
5. wrote
6. taken
7. wrote
8. wrote
9. took
10. wrote
11. took

Lesson 40, Past Tenses of *Give* and *Go* (P. 51)

A. 1. given
2. gone
3. gave
4. went
5. gave
6. gone
7. gave
8. gone
9. gave
10. gone
11. given
12. went
13. given
14. gone
15. given
16. gone

B. 1. went
2. given
3. gone
4. given
5. gone
6. given
7. gone
8. gave
9. went
10. given

Lesson 41, Possessive Pronouns (P. 52)

1. her
2. his
3. their
4. her
5. their
6. his
7. his
8. its
9. their
10. their
11. its
12. his
13. its
14. its
15. her
16. her
17. his
18. its
19. his
20. your
21. his
22. their
23. her
24. his
25. his
26. their

Lesson 42, Indefinite Pronouns (P. 53)

A. 1. Everyone
2. somebody
3. Anything
4. Something
5. Everybody
6. No one
7. anyone
8. Both
9. Nothing
10. anybody
11. Someone
12. Everybody
13. Each
14. Some
15. Several
16. No one
17. Everyone
18. Nobody
19. Everything
20. anything

B. Pronouns will vary.

Lesson 43, Subject Pronouns (P. 54)

1. I
2. She
3. I
4. She
5. I
6. He
7. he
8. She; I
9. I
10. He
11. we
12. They
13. I
14. It
15. You
16. He
17. I
18. She
19. We
20. They
21. she
22. I
23. We
24. we
25. He
26. She
27. I

Lesson 44, Object Pronouns (P. 55)

1. me
2. me
3. her
4. us
5. her
6. them
7. me
8. him
9. him
10. her
11. me
12. us
13. it
14. us
15. them
16. me
17. us
18. him
19. me
20. him
21. them
22. us
23. her
24. him
25. them
26. her
27. us

Lesson 45, Subject Pronouns After Linking Verbs (P. 56)

A.	**1.** I	**5.** she	**9.** he	**13.** he
	2. she	**6.** he	**10.** she	**14.** she
	3. we	**7.** I	**11.** he	**15.** we
	4. they	**8.** she	**12.** they	**16.** I
B.	**1.** they	**4.** she	**7.** she	**10.** she
	2. she	**5.** they	**8.** she	
	3. they	**6.** he	**9.** he	

Lesson 46, Using *Who/Whom* (P. 57)

1. Who	**8.** Whom	**15.** Whom
2. Who	**9.** Whom	**16.** Who
3. Whom	**10.** Whom	**17.** Who
4. Who	**11.** Who	**18.** Whom
5. Who	**12.** Whom	**19.** Who
6. Who	**13.** Who	**20.** Whom
7. Whom	**14.** Who	**21.** Who

Lesson 47, Using Pronouns (P. 58)

1. He; us	**13.** you; him	**25.** We; he
2. you	**14.** you; me; I	**26.** us
3. we	**15.** her; him	**27.** you; I
4. we	**16.** she; them	**28.** You; you; it
5. you; him	**17.** I; you	**29.** they; us
6. She; them	**18.** He; I	**30.** I; them
7. He; me	**19.** They; me	**31.** us
8. Who; you	**20.** Who	**32.** Who
9. I; them	**21.** whom; I	**33.** She; I; you
10. me; she	**22.** I; it; me	**34.** We; them
11. they; us	**23.** She; me	
12. I; her	**24.** They; us	

Lesson 48, More Pronouns (P. 59)

1. I	**13.** our	**25.** We
2. he	**14.** me	**26.** me
3. I	**15.** her	**27.** Who
4. them	**16.** us	**28.** I
5. me	**17.** she	**29.** them
6. me	**18.** Who	**30.** I; his
7. her	**19.** their	**31.** whom
8. Who	**20.** me	**32.** she
9. I	**21.** whom	**33.** she
10. us	**22.** her	**34.** We
11. whom	**23.** us	
12. me	**24.** his	

Lesson 49, Adjectives (P. 60)

A. Adjectives will vary.

B. Adjectives will vary.

Lesson 49, Adjectives (P. 61)

C.	**1.** a	**14.** an	**27.** an	**40.** a
	2. a	**15.** a	**28.** a	**41.** a
	3. a	**16.** an	**29.** a	**42.** an
	4. an	**17.** an	**30.** a	**43.** a
	5. a	**18.** an	**31.** an	**44.** an
	6. an	**19.** an	**32.** an	**45.** an
	7. a	**20.** a	**33.** a	**46.** an
	8. a	**21.** an	**34.** a	**47.** an
	9. a	**22.** a	**35.** a	**48.** a
	10. an	**23.** an	**36.** a	**49.** an
	11. an	**24.** a	**37.** an	**50.** an
	12. an	**25.** an	**38.** an	
	13. a	**26.** an	**39.** an	

Lesson 50, Proper Adjectives (P. 62)

A.	**1.** South American	**10.** Canadian
	2. African	**11.** Norwegian
	3. English	**12.** Scottish
	4. Mexican	**13.** Irish
	5. French	**14.** Chinese
	6. Russian	**15.** Spanish
	7. American	**16.** Italian
	8. Roman	**17.** Hawaiian
	9. Alaskan	**18.** Japanese

B. Sentences will vary.

Lesson 51, Demonstrative Adjectives (P. 63)

A.	**1.** those	**7.** these	**13.** That
	2. these	**8.** these	**14.** that
	3. these	**9.** those	**15.** These
	4. that	**10.** those	**16.** that
	5. this	**11.** those	**17.** this
	6. Those	**12.** those	**18.** This

B. Sentences will vary.

Lesson 52, Comparing with Adjectives (P. 64)

1. smoother; smoothest	**9.** rougher; roughest
2. younger, youngest	**10.** narrower; narrowest
3. sweeter; sweetest	**11.** deeper; deepest
4. stronger; strongest	**12.** shorter; shortest
5. lazier; laziest	**13.** happier; happiest
6. greater; greatest	**14.** colder; coldest
7. kinder, kindest	**15.** prettier; prettiest
8. calmer; calmest	

Lesson 53, More Comparing with Adjectives (P. 65)

A. **1.** more energetic; most energetic
2. more courteous; most courteous
3. more impatient; most impatient
4. more important; most important
5. more difficult; most difficult
6. more wonderful; most wonderful
7. more gracious; most gracious
8. more agreeable; most agreeable

B. **1.** less helpful, least helpful
2. less friendly; least friendly
3. less serious; least serious
4. less agreeable; least agreeable
5. less faithful; least faithful
6. less comfortable; least comfortable
7. less patient; least patient
8. less reliable; least reliable

Lesson 53, More Comparing with Adjectives (P. 66)

C. **1.** nearer
2. tallest
3. more helpful
4. younger
5. most difficult
6. better
7. smallest
8. hottest
9. youngest
10. widest
11. older
12. largest
13. most courteous
14. best
15. coldest
16. more studious
17. taller
18. wealthiest
19. fastest
20. more useful
21. most beautiful
22. narrowest
23. larger
24. best
25. worst
26. most famous
27. most beautiful

Lesson 54, Adverbs (P. 67)

A. Adverbs will vary.

B. Sentences will vary.

Lesson 54, Adverbs (P. 68)

C. **1.** slowly
2. very; quickly
3. too; early
4. patiently
5. very; cautiously
6. always; here
7. very; rapidly
8. swiftly
9. quietly; ahead
10. very; slowly
11. now
12. everywhere
13. extremely
14. always; distinctly
15. far; underwater
16. here
17. quickly
18. very; fast; especially
19. suddenly
20. softly
21. there
22. too; rapidly
23. There; extremely; very
24. politely
25. too; rapidly
26. extremely; well
27. softly
28. carefully
29. wearily
30. very; carefully
31. eagerly
32. recently
33. everywhere; yesterday
34. dearly
35. before
36. badly

Lesson 55, Comparing with Adverbs (P. 69)

1. higher, highest
2. later; latest
3. more slowly; most slowly
4. more clearly; most clearly
5. harder; hardest
6. more quickly; most quickly
7. more beautifully; most beautifully
8. longer; longest

Lesson 56, Using *Doesn't* and *Don't* (P. 70)

1. don't; doesn't
2. doesn't
3. Doesn't
4. Doesn't
5. Doesn't
6. don't
7. Doesn't
8. doesn't
9. doesn't
10. doesn't
11. don't
12. doesn't
13. doesn't
14. don't
15. doesn't
16. doesn't
17. Doesn't
18. doesn't
19. doesn't
20. doesn't
21. Don't
22. doesn't
23. doesn't
24. doesn't
25. don't
26. don't
27. Don't
28. don't

Lesson 57, Using *May/Can* and *Teach/Learn* (P. 71)

A. 1. can 2. can 3. may 4. can 5. can 6. may 7. can 8. can 9. can 10. May

B. 1. teach 2. learn 3. teach 4. learn 5. teach 6. teach 7. teach 8. teach; learn

Lesson 58, Using *Sit/Set* and *Lay/Lie* (P. 72)

A. 1. sit 2. set 3. sit 4. set 5. Set 6. sits 7. set 8. sat 9. sit 10. sit

B. 1. lay 2. Lie 3. lies 4. laid 5. lay 6. lie 7. Lay 8. laid 9. lie 10. lain

Lesson 59, Prepositions (P. 73)

1. on
2. from; with
3. through; toward
4. between
5. for
6. about
7. into
8. to
9. across
10. against
11. over; into
12. across
13. among; of
14. beside
15. across; toward
16. behind
17. around
18. on
19. about; in
20. in
21. to
22. into
23. across
24. of; from
25. among
26. After; to
27. of; in

Lesson 60, Prepositional Phrases (P. 74)

Students should circle words in bold.

1. The founders (of the **United States**) had a vision (of a great **country**).
2. We climbed (into the station **wagon**).
3. Many stars can be seen (on a clear **night**).
4. The top (of my **desk**) has been varnished.
5. Have you ever gone (through a **tunnel**)?
6. Place these memos (on the bulletin **board**).
7. We have a display (of **posters**) (in the **showcase**) (in the **corridor**).
8. Carol, take these reports (to **Ms. Garza**).
9. What is the capital (of **Alabama**)?
10. The fabric (on this antique **sofa**) came (from **France**).
11. Are you a collector (of **minerals**)?
12. I am going (to Julia's **house**).
13. The hillside was dotted (with beautiful wild **flowers**).
14. The rain beat (against the **windowpanes**).
15. We placed a horseshoe (above the **door**).
16. This poem was written (by my oldest **sister**).
17. Great clusters (of **grapes**) hung (from the **vine**).
18. Is he going (to the **race**)?
19. A herd (of **goats**) grazed (on the **hillside**).
20. Are you carrying those books (to the **storeroom**)?
21. Our car stalled (on the **bridge**).
22. My family lives (in **St. Louis**).
23. A small vase (of **flowers**) was placed (in the **center**) (of the **table**).
24. The group sat (around the **fireplace**).
25. The cold wind blew (from the **north**).
26. Doris hit the ball (over the **fence**).
27. The dog played (with the **bone**).
28. High weeds grow (by the narrow **path**).

Lesson 61, Prepositional Phrases as Adjectives/Adverbs (P. 75)

1. to the library; adverb
2. about gardening; adjective
3. in the library; adjective
4. with blue shoes; adjective
5. in the green dress; adjective
6. about the card catalog; adverb
7. for every book; adjective
8. in alphabetical order; adverb
9. in the health section; adverb
10. to the library; adjective
11. with her; adverb
12. at home; adverb
13. in the living room; adjective
14. out the window; adverb
15. by the backyard fence; adjective
16. from last year's garden; adjective
17. near the house; adverb
18. in the summer; adverb

Lesson 62, Conjunctions (P. 76)

A. **1.** until **5.** or **9.** and
2. and **6.** and **10.** for
3. and **7.** Neither, nor
4. or **8.** but

B. Conjunctions will vary. Suggested:
1. until **5.** until **9.** and
2. or **6.** and **10.** Neither; nor
3. and **7.** and
4. and; but **8.** if

Lesson 63, Interjections (P. 77)

Sentences will vary.

Review (P. 78)

A. Students should circle the words in bold.
1. **John Madison** is the president of companies in **Dallas**, **Texas**, and **London**, **England**.
2. **Dr. Margaret Howe** is a professor of business and economics at **Jacksonville University**.
3. Friends and relatives visiting our cabin on **Lake Erie** can enjoy swimming, fishing, boating, and hiking.

B. **1.** magazines **4.** potatoes
2. flashes **5.** elves
3. ponies **6.** stereos

C. **1.** parents' **3.** teachers'
2. children's **4.** singers'

D. **1.** seen **6.** written **11.** I
2. did **7.** gave **12.** us
3. came **8.** doesn't **13.** They
4. took **9.** were **14.** He
5. gone **10.** me **15.** them

Review (P. 79)

E. **1.** me; our **5.** He; she
2. I; her **6.** Who; him
3. us; them **7.** I; his
4. We; their **8.** whom

F. Students should circle the words in bold.
1. This, short, **comfortably**, last
2. The, large, pink
3. Many
4. The, fastest, **easily**, the, finish
5. **carefully**, the, complicated, the, new

G. **1.** youngest **4.** faster
2. louder **5.** taller
3. most beautifully

H. **1.** lay **5.** sit
2. don't **6.** lying
3. learn **7.** doesn't
4. can **8.** teach

I. Students should circle words in bold.
1. Put this basket (of **clothes**) (in the laundry **room**).
2. The hillside was covered (with yellow **daisies**).
3. The top (of the **mountain**) is usually covered (with **snow**).
4. The house (on the **corner**) was sold (in one **week**).

Using What You've Learned (P. 80)

B. Answers will vary.
C. Answers will vary.
D. Answers will vary.
E. Answers will vary.
F. Answers will vary.
G. Answers will vary.

Using What You've Learned (P. 81)

H. In 1585, a group of about 100 men came from England to Roanoke Island to set up a colony. They did not have enough food or supplies. The Native Americans were unfriendly. The group chose to abandon the colony. In 1586, Sir Francis Drake's fleet stopped at the colony and took the men back to England.

The English people would not give up. In 1587, three ships left England. A group of 117 men, women, and children settled on Roanoke Island. They expected to live on the supplies they received from England. In 1590, when the supply ships arrived in Roanoke, the colonists who had come in 1587 had disappeared. The people of Roanoke were never found. Their disappearance is a mystery that has never been solved.

Unit 4 Capitalization and Punctuation

Lesson 64, Using Capital Letters (P. 82)

A. Students should circle and capitalize the first letter in each of the following words:
1. Haven't **5.** Bring
2. The **6.** Who
3. Danielle; How **7.** The; My
4. The **8.** Have

B. Students should circle and capitalize the first letter in each of the following words:
1. I; I've; It; But **5.** Stand; Me
2. It's; Is; The; The **6.** Adam; Road
3. The; Children's; Hour **7.** Chasing; Wind
4. A; Wrinkle; Time

Lesson 64, Using Capital Letters (P. 83)

C. Students should capitalize letters in bold.

chris and her friends went to a festival in **c**hicago **i**llinois. Some of them tasted **g**reek pastry and **c**anadian cheese soup. **c**harley thought that the **i**talian sausage and **m**exican tacos were delicious! **l**aurel tried an unusual **j**apanese salad. They all watched some **i**rish folk dancers and listened to **g**erman music.

D. Students should circle and capitalize the first letter in each of the following words:

1. Anita; Arizona; New; Mexico; Colorado
2. Brazil; United; States
3. Mark; Twain; Hannibal; Missouri
4. Martin; Luther; King
5. Solomon; Islands
6. North; Sea; English; Channel; Strait; Dover
7. Sam; Houston; Tennessee; Lexington; Virginia
8. St.; Augustine; United; States
9. Nairobi; Kenya
10. Japanese

Lesson 64, Using Capital Letters (P. 84)

E. Students should circle and capitalize the first letter in each of the following words:

1. Captain; Cheng; Sergeant; Walters
2. Dr.; Ruth; Banks; Mr.; Juan; Gomez
3. Pres.; Alice; Slater; Mr.; Allen; Norman
4. Principal; Grissom; Mayor; Hadley
5. Halpern; Judge; Patterson
6. Mrs.; Frank; President; Howell
7. Prof.; Mary; Schneider; Dr.; David; Towne
8. Andrew; England
9. Alan; Howell; Supt.; Joyce; Randall

F. Students should circle and capitalize the first letter in each of the following words:

1. Capt. Margaret K. Hansen
2075 Lakeview St.
Phoenix, AZ 85072
2. Jackson School Track Meet
at Wilson Stadium
Tues., Sept. 26, 10:30
649 N. Clark Blvd.
3. Mr. Jonathan Bernt
150 Telson Rd.
Markham, Ontario L3R 1E5
4. Lt. Gary L. Louis
5931 Congress Rd.
Syracuse, NY 13217
5. Thanksgiving Concert
Wed., Nov. 23, 11:00
Practice Tues., Nov. 22, 3:30
See Ms. Evans for details.
6. Gen. David Grimes
329 N. Hayes St.
Louisville, KY 40227

Lesson 65, Using End Punctuation (P. 85)

A.

1. .	**5.** .	**9.** .	**13.** ?
2. ?	**6.** ?	**10.** ?	**14.** .
3. ?	**7.** .	**11.** ?	**15.** .
4. .	**8.** ?	**12.** .	

B.

Line 1. ?	**Line 8.** .
Line 2. ?; .	**Line 9.** .
Line 3. .	**Line 10.** ?
Line 5. .	**Line 11.** .
Line 6. .; ?	**Line 12.** .
Line 7. ?	

Lesson 65, Using End Punctuation (P. 86)

C.

1. .	**5.** .	**9.** .	**13.** !
2. !	**6.** !; .	**10.** !	**14.** ! or .
3. !; .	**7.** .	**11.** ! or .	**15.** .
4. .	**8.** !	**12.** .	**16.** ! or .

D.

Line 1. .	**Line 8.** ! or .; ?
Line 2. ?	**Line 9.** .
Line 3. .; .	**Line 10.** .; .
Line 4. .; !	**Line 11.** ! or .
Line 6. .	**Line 12.** .; ?
Line 7. .	**Line 13.** . or !

Lesson 66, Using Commas (P. 87)

A.

1. The United States exports cotton, corn, and wheat to many countries.
2. The children played softball, ran races, and pitched horseshoes.
3. Lauren held the nail, and Tasha hit it with a hammer.
4. Alice, Henry, Carmen, and James go to the library often.
5. The pitcher threw a fastball, and the batter struck out.
6. Sara peeled the peaches, and Victor sliced them.
7. The mountains were covered with forests of pine, cedar, and oak.
8. Craig should stop running, or he will be out of breath.
9. Baseball is Lee's favorite sport, but Sue's favorite is football.
10. Limestone, marble, granite, and slate are found in Vermont, New Hampshire, and Maine.
11. The rain fell steadily, and the lightning flashed.
12. Mindy enjoyed the corn, but Frank preferred the string beans.

B.

1. "Please show me how this machine works," said Carolyn.
2. "Be sure you keep your eyes on the road," said the driving instructor.
3. Rick replied, "I can't believe my ears."
4. Gail said, "Travel is dangerous on the icy roads."
5. "Paul studied piano for two years," said Ms. Walters.
6. Alex said, "That goat eats everything in sight."
7. "Let's go to the park for a picnic," said Marie.
8. "Wait for me here," said Paul.
9. Tom said, "Sandra, thank you for the present."
10. "I'm going to the game with Al," remarked Frank.
11. Al asked, "What time should we leave?"
12. Chris remembered, "I was only five when we moved to New York."

Lesson 66, Using Commas (P. 88)

C. 1. Miss Hunt, do you know the answer to that question?
2. Can't you find the book I brought you last week, Roger?
3. Dr. Levin, the Smith's dentist, sees patients on weekends.
4. Oh, I guess it takes about an hour to get to Denver.
5. Joe, may Sam and I go to the ball game?
6. Our neighbor, Billy Johnson, is a carpenter.
7. What is the population of your city, Linda?
8. Well, I'm not sure of the exact number.
9. Beth, are you going skiing this weekend?
10. What time are you going to the concert, Greg?
11. Joseph, our friend, coaches the softball team.
12. Sue, have you seen a small black cat around your neighborhood?
13. Jeff, do you know Mr. D. B. Norton?
14. No, I don't think we've ever met.
15. Sally and John, would you like to go shopping on Saturday?
16. Mrs. Porter, the principal, is retiring this year.
17. Yes, the teachers are planning a retirement dinner for her.
18. Mrs. Porter and her husband, Hal, plan to move to Oregon.

D. I have two friends who are always there for me, and I tell them everything. So it was a surprise to me when Carol, my oldest friend, said, "Well, when are you moving?" I said, "What do you mean?" She said, "I don't believe you, our dearest friend, wouldn't tell us first what was going on in your life." Margie, my other friend, said, "I feel the same way. Ann, why on earth did we have to hear about this from Ray?" "Margie and Carol, I don't know what you're talking about," I said. "Oh, don't be ashamed," said Margie. "We know you must have some good reason, and we're waiting to hear it." "No, I don't have any reason because I'm not moving," I said. "Ray, that prankster, must have been trying to play a joke on us," said Carol.

Lesson 67, Using Quotation Marks and Apostrophes (P. 89)

A. 1. "Dan, did you ever play football?" asked Tim.
2. Morris asked, "Why didn't you come in for an interview?"
3. "I have never," said Laurie, "heard a story about a ghost."
4. "Selina," said Yuri, "thank you for the present."
5. "When do we start on our trip to the mountains?" asked Stan.
6. Our guest said, "You don't know how happy I am to be in your house."
7. "My sister," said Kelly, "bought those beautiful baskets in Mexico."
8. "I'm going to plant the spinach," said Doris, "as soon as I get home."

B. 1. players'
2. baby's
3. isn't
4. It's
5. captain's
6. doesn't
7. Men's

Lesson 68, Using Colons and Hyphens (P. 90)

A. 1. 8:30
2. Sanchez:
3. books:
4. 6:15
5. Graham:

B. 1. driving-safety, presen-
2. forty-two
3. zip-
4. mother-in-law
5. fifty-eight
6. ear-
7. twenty-one
8. air-conditioning
9. pup-

Review (P. 91)

Students should circle and capitalize letters in bold.

A. 1. **H**ave you seen **S**helly today?
2. **I**s **M**ajor **B**ill **B**randon your cousin?
3. **M**r. and **M**rs. **J**ohn **B**ell live at the **M**ayflower **A**partments.
4. ***A****lice's* ***A****dventures in* ***W****onderland,* by **L**ewis **C**arroll, is an excellent book.
5. **H**ow do people travel in the deserts of **E**gypt?
6. ***H****eidi* was written by **J**ohanna **S**pyri.
7. **I** can't wait to spend **C**hristmas in **F**lorida with **U**ncle **W**ill and **A**unt **L**ee.
8. **M**onticello is the beautiful home of **T**homas **J**efferson, near **C**harlottesville, **V**irginia.
9. ***J****ungle* ***B****ook* was written by **R**udyard **K**ipling.
10. **F**lorida produces more oranges than any other state in the **U**nited **S**tates.
11. "**I** am sure she lives at 203 **L**incoln **A**venue," replied **S**andra.
12. **M**r. **B**aldwin, you won a trip to **B**ermuda!
13. "**T**he **S**tar **S**pangled **B**anner" was written by **F**rancis **S**cott **K**ey.
14. **M**rs. **P**erkins has written many interesting stories about the **C**anadian, **A**laskan, and **N**ative **A**merican people.
15. **I**sn't **M**ount **E**verest the highest mountain in the world?
16. **H**ave you ever crossed the **R**ocky **M**ountains?
17. **H**ow many miles does the **S**t. **L**awrence **R**iver flow?
18. **O**ne hundred **F**rench tourists were on the guided tour of **W**ashington, **D**.**C**.
19. **S**ometime **I** want to visit **M**exico **C**ity.
20. **C**arol **R**. **B**rink wrote a book about a boy in **S**cotland.
21. **T**he first **M**onday in **S**eptember is known as **L**abor **D**ay.
22. **T**he **O**lympic team will leave for **P**aris, **F**rance, on **T**hanksgiving **D**ay.

Review (P. 92)

B. **1.** Tom, do you know where the paper, pencils, and test forms are?
2. "We really enjoyed our trip through Florida, Georgia, and South Carolina," said Mr. Shaw.
3. I gave Angela, my niece, a pair of skates for her birthday, and her parents gave her a radio.
4. "Jason, please wash, dry, and fold the laundry for me," said Connie.
5. Dr. Wells, our family doctor, is retiring, but Dr. Hernandez will take over her practice.
6. Yes, I think Ms. Lawson, my supervisor, is a courteous, capable, and fair person.
7. I want to go to the beach on our vacation, but my friend wants to go camping, hiking, and fishing.
8. Do you want to go to a movie or play cards, Sharonda?
9. Mr. Coe, my English instructor, said, "Make sure your reports are neat, concise, and accurate."
10. Dawn told Ms. Mendez, a nurse, about Kelsey's fever.
11. James will mow the yard, trim the hedge, and water the flowers.
12. Sara Powell, the district attorney, will look into the case.

C. **1.** My mother-in-law said, "Mary's aunt will join us for dinner at 7:30."
2. Rosa couldn't find the following items for her trip: suntan lotion, her hat, and the keys to the cabin.
3. "Juan," asked Linda, "will you please bring forty-eight cookies for the club's bake sale?"
4. Ms. Tyson's secretary began the letter with "Dear Sir: I am writing on behalf of Ms. Tyson."
5. Scott said, "I'm going to Jim's house tonight at 8:00 to help him finish his son's desk."
6. Meg's friends gave her many gifts at her good-bye party: a new shirt, two headbands, stationery, and a roll of stamps.
7. "Mike and Todd don't have to go to bed until 9:30," said Larry.
8. Mr. Reid's son is only twenty-one years old and is already a well-known figure in the com-munity.
9. Rita said, "The beautiful memorial fountain is near the park's main entrance."
10. "Won't you be taking the coach's extra-credit class?" asked Eric.
11. Stephanie's party begins at 8:30.
12. "What time is your appointment, Jack?" asked Diane.

Using What You've Learned (P. 93)

A. Students should circle letters in bold.

one of **a**esop's fables is called "**t**he **f**ox and the **c**row." **i**t tells about a crow that stole a piece of cheese. **t**he crow landed on the branch of a tree, put the cheese in her mouth, and began to eat it. **b**ut a fox was also interested in the cheese. **h**e sat under the branch, and he thought about eating the cheese, too.

the fox said, "**c**row, **i** compliment you on your size, beauty, and strength. **y**ou would be the queen of all birds if you had a voice."

"**c**aw!" exclaimed the crow.

well, the crow dropped the cheese. **t**he fox pounced on it, carried it off a few feet, and then turned around.

"**m**y friend," said the fox, "you have every good quality except common sense."

our neighbor, **d**enise **b**aldwin, likes to tell me funny stories. **o**ne hot **f**riday afternoon in **a**ugust she told me about her trip to **a**tlanta, **g**eorgia. **s**he was walking out of a store with some presents she had bought for **p**at, her sister. **t**hey were three joke gifts which included the following: birthday candles that didn't blow out, a silly hat, and a mustache attached to some glasses. **d**enise accidentally bumped into another shopper.

"**i**'m so sorry!" exclaimed **d**enise.

"**a**re you hurt?" asked the other shopper.

"**n**o, **i**'m not hurt," said **d**enise. **b**oth shoppers had dropped their presents, and they bent over to pick them up.

"**i**'m **d**enise **b**aldwin," she said as she picked up the presents.

"**m**y name is **c**arol **s**chwartz," said the other shopper.

both shoppers said they were sorry again and then went on their way.

denise gave her sister the presents when she returned to **m**iami, **f**lorida. **p**at had a puzzled look on her face when she unwrapped them. **t**he packages contained a rattle, a bib, and a baby bonnet!

"**o**h!" gasped **d**enise. "**i** must have picked up the wrong presents when **i** bumped into **m**s. **s**chwartz."

"**w**ho's **m**s. **s**chwartz?" asked **p**at.

denise laughed and said, "**i** hope she's someone who likes joke gifts!"

Using What You've Learned (P. 94)

B. Sir Walter Scott, one of the world's greatest storytellers, was born in Edinburgh, Scotland, on August 15, 1771. Walter had an illness just before he was two years old that left him lame for the rest of his life. His par-ents were worried, so they sent him to his grandparents' farm in Sandy Knowe. They thought the country air would do him good.

Walter's parents were right. He was quite healthy by the time he was six years old. He was happy, too. Walter loved listening to his grandfather tell stories about Scotland. The stories stirred his imagination. He began to read fairy tales, travel books, and history books. It was these ear-ly stories that laid the groundwork for Scott's later interest in writing stories. His most famous book, *Ivanhoe*, has been read by people around the world.

Unit 5 Composition

Lesson 69, Writing Sentences (P. 95)

A. Sentences will vary.

B. Sentences will vary.

Lesson 70, Writing Topic Sentences (P. 96)

A. Topic sentences will vary.

B. Topic sentences will vary.

Lesson 71, Writing Supporting Details (P. 97)

A. Students should circle numbers 1, 3, 4, 5, 7, 8, 10.

B. Sentences will vary.

Lesson 72, Topic and Audience (P. 98)

A. Answers will vary.

B. Answers will vary.

C. Paragraphs will vary.

Lesson 73, Taking Notes (P. 99)

A. Answers will vary.

B. Topics and notes will vary.

Lesson 74, Outlining (P. 100)

Outlines will vary.

Lesson 75, Writing a Report (P. 101)

B. 1. facts
2. diameter
3. Mars

C. The planets Uranus . . . from Earth.
Scientists . . . of Uranus.
Scientists . . . of Neptune.
It was 1930 . . . was discovered.
There are more . . . about Pluto.
Many mysteries . . . been discovered.

Lesson 76, Revising and Proofreading (P. 102)

A. Yellowstone National Park is the oldest and largest national park in the United States. It is located partly in northwestern Wyoming, partly in southern Montana, and partly in eastern Idaho. During the summer of 1988, large parts of the park were damaged by fire. A serious lack of rain was part of the reason the fire was so severe. One fire threatened to destroy the park's famous lodge, which is constructed entirely of wood. Fortunately, firefighters' efforts saved the lodge from destruction. Today the forests are slowly recovering from the fires.

Lesson 76, Revising and Proofreading (P. 103)

B. ¶ although yellowstons national park is the largest ~~national~~ national park in the United states, other national parks are also well-known yosemite national park in california has acres of Mountain Scenery and miles of hiking trails. Won of the world's largest ~~biggest~~ waterfalls can also be found in yosemite.

¶ mammoth cave national park in kentucky features a huge underground cave the cave over has 212 miles of corridors it also ~~have~~ has underground lakes rivers and waterfalls this cave system is estimated to be millions of years old

¶ many pepul are surprized to learn that their are national parks in alaska and hawaii. mount McKinley the highest mountain in north america is located in denali national park in alaska. you can travel to hawaii and visit hawaii volcanoes national park this Park Has too active volcanoes rare plants and animals.

Although Yellowstone National Park is the largest national park in the United States, other national parks are also well-known. Yosemite National Park in California has acres of mountain scenery and miles of hiking trails. One of the world's largest waterfalls can also be found in Yosemite.

Mammoth Cave National Park in Kentucky features a huge underground cave. The cave has over 212 miles of corridors. It also has underground lakes, rivers, and waterfalls. This cave system is estimated to be millions of years old.

Many people are surprised to learn that there are national parks in Alaska and Hawaii. Mount McKinley, the highest mountain in North America, is located in Denali National Park in Alaska. You can travel to Hawaii and visit Hawaii Volcanoes National Park. This park has two active volcanoes, rare plants, and animals.

Lesson 77, Writing a Business Letter (P. 104)

A. **1.** Chris Morrow
2. Dear Sir or Madam:
3. 9940 Main Street, Brooklyn, NY 11227
4. April 4, 1994

Lesson 77, Writing a Business Letter (P. 105)

B. Letters will vary. Students should circle the addresses.

Review (P. 106)

A. Sentences will vary.

B. Topic sentences will vary.

C. Topic sentences will vary.

D. **1.** a, c
2. a, b
3. a, c

Review (P. 107)

E. Notes and outlines will vary.

F. Flying a kite can be fun, but it can also serve some practical purposes. For example, Benjamin franklin uses a kite in his experiments with electricity. In the early part of the twentieth century, box kites carring instruments measured wind speed temperature pressure ~~and~~ and humidity. they were also used to lift soldiers to hieghts where they could see the enemy. Today they serve as signals in air-see-rescue operations.

G. **1.** 4 **4.** 2
2. 5 **5.** 3
3. 1 **6.** 6

Using What You've Learned (P. 108)

A. Reports will vary.

Using What You've Learned (P. 109)

B. Reports and revisions will vary.

Unit 6 Study Skills

Lesson 78, Dictionary: Guide Words (P. 110)

A. Students should check the following words:

1. fruit, furnish, gate, gallon, fuzz, galaxy, future
2. muddy, moss, motorcycle, moose, morning, mortal
3. perfume, pick, photo, pest, pillow, pile

B. Students should number the words as follows:

1. rabbit / remind	**2.** scent / silent	**3.** occasion / only
2	3	2
3	8	9
1	9	5
5	11	6
7	12	8
9	1	4
8	10	10
4	7	7
11	6	3
12	4	11
10	2	1
6	5	12

Lesson 79, Dictionary: Syllables (P. 111)

A. **1.** advertise **5.** concrete
2. blunder **6.** microphone
3. paradise **7.** incident
4. mischievous **8.** value

B. **1.** bi-cy-cle **8.** the-o-ry
2. so-lu-tion **9.** won-der-ful
3. cat-e-go-ry **10.** bi-ol-o-gy
4. pun-ish-ment **11.** siz-zle
5. be-hav-ior **12.** for-eign
6. quar-ter-back **13.** trans-par-ent
7. dis-ap-pear **14.** civ-i-li-za-tion

C. **1.** mos-quito mosqui-to
2. am-bition ambi-tion
3. bound-ary bounda-ry
4. ginger-bread gin-gerbread
5. Answers will vary.
6. leader-ship lead-ership

Lesson 80, Dictionary: Pronunciation (P. 112)

A. 1. at
2. 5
3. Answers will vary.
4. hw
5. rüle
6. th

B. 1. alive
2. load
3. true
4. thick
5. fallen
6. cape
7. ice
8. they
9. supper
10. locker
11. home
12. fought
13. might
14. fool
15. freeze
16. lettuce

Lesson 81, Dictionary: Definitions and Parts of Speech (P. 113)

1. speckle
2. specify
3. specimen
4. spectacular
5. Sentences will vary.
6. Sentences will vary.
7. Sentences will vary.
8. Sentences will vary.
9. spectacular
10. specimen

Lesson 82, Dictionary: Word Origins (P. 114)

1. wampum
2. strings of money
3. pasteurize
4. chaise longue
5. chair; long
6. gardenia
7. wampum
8. campus, gardenia
9. utter
10. taxes
11. utter
12. out
13. field
14. gardenia
15. chaise longue

Lesson 83, Using Parts of a Book (P. 115)

A. 1. copyright page
2. index
3. title page
4. table of contents

B. 1. 1995
2. Steck-Vaughn Company
3. Austin, TX
4. 110
5. 29
6. Lesson 77, Writing a Business Letter
7. 82, 83, 84
8. 53
9. Lesson 6, Contractions
10. Vocabulary
11. Possessive Nouns
12. 14
13. Study Skills
14. 106
15. Past Tenses of *Blow* and *Fly*

Lesson 84, Using the Library (P. 116)

A. 1. 600–699
2. 400–499
3. 000–099
4. 900–999
5. 100–199
6. 200–299
7. 500–599
8. 800–899
9. 700–799
10. 300–399
11. 400–499
12. 500–599
13. 600–699
14. 800–899
15. 900–999

B. Answers will vary.

Lesson 85, Using the Card Catalog (P. 117)

A. 1. Hoobler, Dorothy and Thomas
2. Images across the ages: African portraits
3. 96
4. 920.067 H66
5. 1993
6. African history

B. 1. subject
2. title
3. author
4. subject
5. author
6. title

Lesson 86, Using an Encyclopedia (P. 118)

1. Clarence Birdseye
2. 1886–1956
3. Amherst College
4. developing methods of preserving foods, and marketing quick-frozen foods
5. lighting technology, wood-pulping methods, and heating processes
6. food processing
7. Answers will vary.
8. no

Lesson 87, Finding an Encyclopedia Article (P. 119)

A. 1. 3
2. 14
3. 19
4. 16
5. 14
6. 11
7. 11
8. 7
9. 14
10. 17
11. 3
12. 19
13. 9
14. 6
15. 15

B. Answers will vary.

C. Answers will vary.

Lesson 88, Using Visual Aids (P. 120)

1. Terry
2. Julia, Miguel, and Terry
3. Miguel
4. Ted
5. graph
6. chart

Lesson 88, Using Visual Aids (P. 121)

1. south
2. Walnut Street and Oak Street
3. school
4. Riverside Drive
5. Pine Street
6. north
7. north and south
8. about 7 miles, or 11 kilometers

Lesson 89, Using a Thesaurus (P. 122)

A. 1. heat
2. warmth, fire, flame, fever, emotion, glow, blush, redness
3. flame
4. fever
5. cold, coolness, ice, chilliness
6. coolness, chilliness
7. cold

B. 1. fire
2. warmth
3. glow
4. redness
5. fever
6. flame
7. blush
8. emotion

Lesson 90, Choosing Reference Sources (P. 123)

1. dictionary
2. dictionary, encyclopedia, or atlas
3. encyclopedia
4. atlas
5. encyclopedia
6. encyclopedia
7. dictionary
8. dictionary
9. encyclopedia
10. encyclopedia or atlas
11. encyclopedia
12. dictionary
13. encyclopedia or atlas
14. encyclopedia
15. encyclopedia or atlas
16. encyclopedia
17. dictionary
18. encyclopedia or atlas
19. dictionary
20. encyclopedia

Review (P. 124)

A. 1. noun
2. 1
3. 2
4. twin
5. tuxedo
6. 3; 1
7. noun, adjective, verb
8. c. tusk/twirl

B. 1. table of contents
2. title page
3. copyright page
4. index

C. 1. by call numbers
2. author, title, subject
3. author card

Review (P. 125)

D. 1. New; countries
2. South; states
3. palm; trees

E. 1. west
2. about 4 miles, or 5 kilometers
3. north

F. 1. sweet
2. pleasant, pure, fresh, sugary
3. pleasant

G. 1. dictionary
2. atlas or encyclopedia
3. encyclopedia

Using What You've Learned (P. 126)

A. Answers will vary.

B. Answers will vary.

C. 1. b (subject card)
2. Fiona MacDonald
3. New view: Rain forest
4. Raintree/ Steck-Vaughn
5. yes
6. 574.5 M235

Using What You've Learned (P. 127)

D. 1. Answers will vary.
2. Answers will vary.
3. Cross-references will vary.

E. 1. Jeff and Lupe
2. Steve
3. Lupe
4. chart

Final Reviews

Final Review, Unit 1 (P. 128)

1. A	**6.** S	**11.** A
2. S	**7.** A	**12.** A
3. S	**8.** S	**13.** S
4. S	**9.** A	**14.** S
5. A	**10.** S	**15.** S

1. stakes	**3.** bore	**5.** bread	**7.** plane
2. meet	**4.** needs	**6.** son	**8.** heard

Sentences will vary.

Final Review, Unit 1 (P. 129)

1. impossible
2. successful
3. rewrite
4. uncertain

1. Where is; air/plane
2. it is; down/town
3. Is not; head/quarters
4. they are; high/rise

1. homely
2. old
3. raved
4. fascinating

Sentences will vary.

1. hit the sack
2. left high and dry
3. up in the air
4. all thumbs

Final Review, Unit 2 (P. 130)

1. E; ! or D; .	**7.** IM; .
2. IN;?	**8.** IN; ?
3. X	**9.** X
4. IN; ?	**10.** E; ! or D; .
5. X	**11.** E; !
6. D; .	**12.** D; .

Students should circle Sentence 8.

1. Bicycling / is . . .
2. Cyclists / can learn . . .
3. cyclists / wear . . .
4. helmet / is . . .
5. Experts / recommend . . .
6. riders / should learn . . .
7. people / should obey . . .
8. Are / you . . .

1. CP, John Scott / is . . .
2. CS, His wife and two children / ride . . .
3. CS, John and his wife / run . . .
4. CP, The Scott children / visit . . .
5. CP, The Scott family / helps . . .
6. CS, Victoria and Nick Scott / think . . .

Final Review, Unit 2 (P. 131)

1. A bicycle safety course is offered at our neighborhood center, and the class is for children and adults together.
2. People are taught important traffic rules, and they learn ways to prevent bicycle thefts.
3. Everyone must pass a final bicycling test, because they will not get a certificate if they fail.

Sentences will vary.

Final Review, Unit 3 (P. 132)

1. n., v., pp.
2. adj., n., adv.
3. int., adj., adv.
4. conj., pron., v., pp.
5. pp., v., pron., n., prep.
6. n., adj., n., pp.
7. pron., v., adj., n.
8. adj., pron., adj., adj.

1. were	**6.** drank	**11.** broken
2. completed	**7.** eaten	**12.** grew
3. seen	**8.** rang	**13.** gone
4. came	**9.** sung	**14.** given
5. done	**10.** chosen	**15.** written

Final Review, Unit 3 (P. 133)

Answers will vary. Sample paragraphs follow:

Trees are important for their products and their benefits to the environment. Wood is one of the main building supplies in the world and an important fuel. Paper and paper products are made from wood pulp. Trees also produce various nuts and fruits for both animals and humans.

One way trees help the environment is by releasing oxygen into the air. For instance, if a tree has taken in sunlight and carbon dioxide, it will release oxygen. Tree roots help control erosion and flooding. Trees have always given homes for shelter for many animals. Raccoons, squirrels, and other animals make their homes in trees.

Many trees have lived and grown for thousands of years and are hundreds of feet tall. The redwoods in California are some of the tallest trees in the world. The tallest tree is 364 feet tall and lives in Humboldt National Forest. The oldest living tree is a bristlecone pine in Nevada that is over 4,600 years old.

Final Review, Unit 4 (P. 134)

Students should circle and capitalize the first letter in each of the following words. Students should also add end punctuation.

1. How; ?; Marie
2. Her; .
3. It's; !; Peter
4. Marie; Peter; George; .
5. I; George; .
6. I'd; Marie; .
7. Then; ?; Peter
8. Marie; .
9. That's; !
10. Peter; George; Marie; .

122 E. Park Street
Denver, CO 81442
October 10, 1994

Mr. Marshall Chase
3910 Prairie Avenue
Lowell, MA 01740

Dear Mr. Chase:

Thank you very much for your interest in my star-gazing book, *A Guide to the Stars.* I published it in September through a well-known astronomy publisher, The Sky's the Limit Press. According to my publisher, books will be available at bookstores this month.

I have the answer to your question on how I do my research. I have a very powerful telescope that I use every day. I do most of my work at night between 10:15 P.M. and 1:30 A.M. I find those to be the darkest hours out here in Colorado. Finally, I have a piece of advice for budding astronomers. Always keep a journal of the stars you see each night, and try to memorize their location. I always say to my students, "The sky's the limit!" Good luck star-gazing.

Sincerely,
Professor Liz Nelson

Final Review, Unit 4 (P. 135)

Ted Carter, a United Nations spokesperson, announced, "Many remote towns and villages in Mexico have been destroyed by a major earthquake, and the United States and Canada are sending emergency relief. International troops will help with fires, flooding, and injuries resulting from the earthquake." The spokesperson further stated, "Colonel Marks, commander of relief troops, will oversee medical staff, rescue crews, and cleanup operations." Mr. Carter said, "The troops will provide medical supplies, food, water, and temporary shelter for the earthquake victims." He ended his statement by saying, "The troops are preparing now, and they should begin arriving in Mexico tomorrow morning." Mr. Carter then told the reporters that he would answer some questions.

"Mr. Carter, are any more countries involved in the relief efforts?" asked Dorian Kramer, reporter for the *Richland Register.*

Mr. Carter replied, "Yes. England, France, and Germany are also sending supplies and medical staff."

Pete Simmons, KRSS reporter, asked, "How long will our troops be in Mexico?"

Mr. Carter responded, "Well, the President is not sure, but we expect the troops to be there several weeks."

Joe Kelly, *Up-Date* magazine reporter, asked, "How many deaths and injuries have been reported?"

"We do not have exact figures, but we know there are many people hurt and missing," said Mr. Carter.

1. The boys' father didn't want them to stay home alone.
2. Of all the countries I've visited, these countries' scenery impressed me most: England, France, and Switzerland.
3. The flowers' petals weren't as colorful as the pictures showed them to be.
4. The Los Angeles mayor's speeches at the national mayors' convention will be at these times: 5:00 P.M., 7:30 P.M., and 9:00 P.M.
5. My house's roof wasn't damaged by hail, but other houses' roofs were: Jim's roof, my father-in-law's roof, my cousin's roof, and Ms. Brown's roof.
6. Many children attend our public library's children's hour on Tuesdays from 9:00 A.M. to 10:00 A.M.
7. The new store's advertisement said it specializes in men's and women's clothing, ladies' jew-elry, and perfumes from around the world.
8. The winner's trophy will be awarded to one out of the twenty-two contestants.

Final Review, Unit 5 (P. 136)

Topic sentences and audiences will vary.

1. a, b
2. a, c
3. b, c

Final Review, Unit 5 (P. 137)

Did you know that roughly three-quarters of the earth's fresh water is not held in rivers and lakes? The water is held in glaciers, large sheets of ice that form in high altitudes and polar regions such as Antarctica and Greenland. There are between 70,000 and 200,000 glaciers in the world.

As temperatures warm, glaciers melt a little and move at a rate that can't be seen. As they move, they sometimes freeze and add to their mass before moving on. They actually reshape the land they pass over. The most famous glaciers are in Europe. The best-known ones are in the French and Swiss Alps.

Final Review, Unit 6 (P. 138)

1. c. (fire / flight)
2. 3; 2
3. noun
4. 1
5. (flēt); (furm)
6. firm

1. table of contents
2. index
3. copyright page
4. title page

1. atlas or encyclopedia
2. dictionary
3. encyclopedia
4. thesaurus or dictionary
5. atlas or encyclopedia
6. encyclopedia
7. dictionary or thesaurus
8. dictionary

Final Review, Unit 6 (P. 139)

1. Philip Arthur Sauvain
2. 302.2 S28
3. 1990
4. Raintree/Steck-Vaughn

1. Tuesday and Thursday
2. Friday
3. Wednesday
4. graph

Tests

TEST: Unit 1, Pages 29–30, Teacher's Guide

1. D
2. A
3. B
4. C
5. B
6. C
7. D
8. A
9. C
10. B
11. C
12. B
13. D
14. A
15. C
16. B
17. D
18. B
19. C
20. A
21. A
22. D
23. B
24. C
25. C
26. B
27. B
28. D
29. B
30. A
31. C
32. B
33. A
34. C
35. B
36. B

TEST: Unit 2, Pages 31–32, Teacher's Guide

1. B
2. A
3. D
4. C
5. B
6. A
7. A
8. C
9. D
10. B
11. A
12. B
13. C
14. D
15. C
16. A
17. A
18. C
19. B
20. D
21. C
22. A
23. B
24. C
25. A
26. B
27. C
28. A
29. A
30. C
31. C
32. A

TEST: Unit 3, Pages 33–34 , Teacher's Guide

1. A
2. B
3. C
4. B
5. B
6. B
7. B
8. D
9. C
10. C
11. B
12. A
13. C
14. A
15. A
16. B
17. B
18. A
19. C
20. A
21. C
22. B
23. C
24. A
25. B
26. C
27. C
28. A
29. B
30. B
31. C
32. B
33. C
34. A
35. A
36. C
37. B
38. A
39. A
40. C
41. B
42. A
43. C

TEST: Unit 4, Pages 35–36, Teacher's Guide

1. C
2. D
3. D
4. B
5. C
6. A
7. A
8. B
9. C
10. A
11. B
12. C
13. A
14. C
15. B
16. C
17. C
18. A
19. C
20. A
21. B
22. B
23. C
24. A
25. A
26. A
27. B
28. B

TEST: Unit 5, Pages 37–38, Teacher's Guide

1. C
2. D
3. C
4. A
5. B
6. B
7. D
8. B
9. D
10. B
11. D
12. D
13. C
14. D

TEST: Unit 6, Page 39–40, Teacher's Guide

1. A
2. C
3. B
4. A
5. B
6. B
7. C
8. A
9. B
10. C
11. A
12. B
13. A
14. C
15. C
16. B
17. A
18. B
19. D
20. A
21. D
22. C
23. B
24. D
25. A
26. B
27. C

Choose whether the underlined words in each sentence are synonyms, antonyms, homonyms, or homographs.

1. If you duck your head under here, you can see the baby duck.
   A ○ synonyms B ○ antonyms C ○ homonyms D ○ homographs
2. Please show me how to operate the lawn mower, so I can use it properly.
   A ○ synonyms B ○ antonyms C ○ homonyms D ○ homographs
3. My friend asked me a question, but I told him I didn't know the answer.
   A ○ synonyms B ○ antonyms C ○ homonyms D ○ homographs
4. The perfume she sent has a wonderful scent.
   A ○ synonyms B ○ antonyms C ○ homonyms D ○ homographs
5. Don't worry about something that's not real; nothing will come of it.
   A ○ synonyms B ○ antonyms C ○ homonyms D ○ homographs
6. Even though its leg is hurt, it's not broken.
   A ○ synonyms B ○ antonyms C ○ homonyms D ○ homographs
7. Can you reach that can of peaches on the top shelf?
   A ○ synonyms B ○ antonyms C ○ homonyms D ○ homographs
8. The brave soldiers won their battle, and they won medals for their fearless deeds.
   A ○ synonyms B ○ antonyms C ○ homonyms D ○ homographs
9. They're going to their cabin for vacation.
   A ○ synonyms B ○ antonyms C ○ homonyms D ○ homographs
10. Before you begin the next topic, please let me finish taking notes on this one.
    A ○ synonyms B ○ antonyms C ○ homonyms D ○ homographs

Add a prefix or suffix to the underlined word to make a new word that makes sense in the sentence.

11. It is possible to sleep in at my house.
    A ○ pre- C ○ im-
    B ○ un- D ○ -ity
12. We spend end hours talking together.
    A ○ un- C ○ -ful
    B ○ -less D ○ -ous
13. Please move your shoes before entering.
    A ○ un- C ○ -y
    B ○ -able D ○ re-
14. Be care not to disturb the baby.
    A ○ -ful C ○ -able
    B ○ -less D ○ mis-

Name ______________________

15. The train traveled stop to Chicago.

A ○ dis-
B ○ -able
C ○ non-
D ○ mis-

16. She had a remark way of explaining.

A ○ un-
B ○ -able
C ○ -ness
D ○ mis-

17. That country is very mountain.

A ○ -al
B ○ -ness
C ○ -able
D ○ -ous

18. He placed his new hat.

A ○ un-
B ○ mis-
C ○ non-
D ○ -able

19. We enjoyed the movie view.

A ○ -al
B ○ dis-
C ○ pre-
D ○ un-

20. We take an occasion trip.

A ○ -al
B ○ -ous
C ○ un-
D ○ -y

Choose the correct contraction for each pair of underlined words.

21. you would

A ○ you'd
B ○ you'ld
C ○ y'oud
D ○ youd'

22. they are

A ○ there
B ○ their
C ○ theyr'e
D ○ they're

23. it is

A ○ its'
B ○ it's
C ○ ites
D ○ its

24. will not

A ○ win't
B ○ wo'nt
C ○ won't
D ○ willn't

25. I will

A ○ I'm
B ○ I've
C ○ I'll
D ○ I'd

26. does not

A ○ didn't
B ○ doesn't
C ○ don't
D ○ does'nt

Add a word to each underlined word to make it a compound word.

27. We took the ferry to the island.

A ○ tale
B ○ boat
C ○ man
D ○ route

28. She could not stand him.

A ○ by
B ○ head
C ○ grand
D ○ under

Choose whether each underlined word has a positive connotation (+), a negative connotation (−), or is neutral (N).

29. This dress is cheap. A ○ (+) B ○ (−) C ○ (N)

30. My sister is very slender. A ○ (+) B ○ (−) C ○ (N)

31. Tom will walk with us. A ○ (+) B ○ (−) C ○ (N)

32. The movie was disgusting. A ○ (+) B ○ (−) C ○ (N)

33. The heroine was brave. A ○ (+) B ○ (−) C ○ (N)

34. Did you ask your doctor? A ○ (+) B ○ (−) C ○ (N)

Choose the correct meaning for each idiom.

35. beside herself

A ○ out of favor
B ○ very upset
C ○ unable to decide
D ○ in a difficult situation

36. walking on air

A ○ accept defeat
B ○ extremely happy
C ○ meet by chance
D ○ be in trouble

 Name ____________________

Choose the phrase that is not a sentence.

1. A ○ Here we go!
   B ○ Having fun now.
   C ○ Let's go eat.
   D ○ Will you come?

2. A ○ In a minute.
   B ○ She was sleeping.
   C ○ The storm ended.
   D ○ Don't go alone.

3. A ○ You should see that!
   B ○ Why are you here?
   C ○ Do the right thing.
   D ○ For my friend.

4. A ○ He said nothing.
   B ○ It was old.
   C ○ Fine for her.
   D ○ The dog barked.

Choose (A) if the group of words is an interrogative sentence, (B) if it is an imperative sentence, (C) if it is an exclamatory sentence, or (D) if it is a declarative sentence.

5. Be careful with that. A ○ B ○ C ○ D ○
6. When did you go? A ○ B ○ C ○ D ○
7. Why did you leave? A ○ B ○ C ○ D ○
8. What a wonderful day it is! A ○ B ○ C ○ D ○
9. I must show her. A ○ B ○ C ○ D ○
10. Don't drop that. A ○ B ○ C ○ D ○
11. Would they come? A ○ B ○ C ○ D ○
12. Be there by noon. A ○ B ○ C ○ D ○
13. He is such a nice person! A ○ B ○ C ○ D ○
14. I'll go down by the river. A ○ B ○ C ○ D ○
15. I was so surprised! A ○ B ○ C ○ D ○
16. What did you say? A ○ B ○ C ○ D ○

Choose each sentence that has a line drawn between the complete subject and the complete predicate.

17. A ○ My sister Claire/likes to swim in the lake before breakfast.
    B ○ Sam will/clean the fish that we catch today.
    C ○ My brother and sister are/cleaning the sailboat.
    D ○ Janice saw/Steven at the lake.

18. A ○ The seasons are the/four divisions of the year.
    B ○ The origin/of the wheat plant is uncertain.
    C ○ Yosemite National Park/is very popular.
    D ○ Many towns/in the United States are built near water.

19. A ○ I like to study/chemistry and biology.
    B ○ My sister/graduated from college last year.
    C ○ Many/tourists visit Paris, France each year.
    D ○ The railroad passes through/the middle of the city.

20. A ○ My friends and I went to/London last summer.
    B ○ The doctor said it's/nothing to worry about.
    C ○ I really like the/new computer you bought.
    D ○ Pamela/has been sick for three days.

Name ______________________________

Choose the sentence in which the simple subject is underlined.

21. A ○ They caught all kinds of fish.
    B ○ My dog has fleas.
    C ○ This is my favorite tool.
    D ○ Her only brother is visiting.

22. A ○ The warm climate attracts visitors.
    B ○ The people boarded a train.
    C ○ The tall pine trees hid the cabin.
    D ○ She filled the vase with flowers.

Choose the sentence in which the simple predicate is underlined.

23. A ○ Jerry closed the store early.
    B ○ Karen has been on vacation.
    C ○ Jacob can play the flute.
    D ○ We saw them yesterday.

24. A ○ She spoke politely.
    B ○ The first game will be tomorrow.
    C ○ Our program is starting soon.
    D ○ The handle broke in half.

Choose the sentence that is in inverted order.

25. A ○ Down came the rain.
    B ○ She fell on the ice.
    C ○ The cat scratched the chair.
    D ○ The judge is coming.

26. A ○ Tell me about it.
    B ○ How did that happen?
    C ○ We went up the stairs .
    D ○ The dish fell and broke.

Choose the sentence that has a compound subject.

27. A ○ Fred went fishing and hiking.
    B ○ The boys waded out into the stream.
    C ○ Carla and Rudy cooked dinner.
    D ○ The storm howled and raged.

Choose the sentence that has a compound predicate.

28. A ○ She made and wrapped all her presents.
    B ○ The clerk added up the numbers.
    C ○ He turned around slowly.
    D ○ Thirty men and women enrolled.

Choose the sentence that is a compound sentence.

29. A ○ I would like to go, but I can't.
    B ○ Last night, we saw Pete and Sara at the movie theater.
    C ○ Jane and Josie will help Zachary wash the car tomorrow.
    D ○ Would you like fish or chicken for lunch, Ladonna?

30. A ○ Yes, I prefer to go home.
    B ○ She wanted to go to the first game of the season.
    C ○ You can go with him, or you can stay with me.
    D ○ Since when do you like to watch football?

Choose the sentence that is a run-on sentence.

31. A ○ My grandfather works as a janitor at a hospital.
    B ○ He enjoys working with his hands, and he likes to meet new people.
    C ○ He once fixed our furnace, it's worked well ever since.
    D ○ My mom says that I got my common sense from Grandpa.

32. A ○ Have you ever seen the Statue of Liberty, it's in New York?
    B ○ The statue is copper, and it was given to the U.S. by France in 1884.
    C ○ The statue's official name is Liberty Enlightening the World.
    D ○ Each year, approximately two million people visit the Statue of Liberty.

 Name ______________________

TEST Unit 3

Choose which kind of noun is underlined in each sentence.

1. Our vacation was wonderful. A ○ common B ○ proper C ○ possessive
2. The judge told Mr. Clark he was free to go. A ○ common B ○ proper C ○ possessive
3. My brother's ranch is in Wyoming. A ○ common B ○ proper C ○ possessive

Choose the correct form of the noun.

4. singular A ○ men B ○ man C ○ men's
5. possessive A ○ brush B ○ brush's C ○ brushes
6. plural A ○ horse B ○ horses C ○ horse's

Choose each sentence with an appositive.

7. A ○ James, please bake my favorite dessert.
   B ○ He told Eric, his brother, to be careful.
   C ○ Did you borrow my hat, Sharon?
   D ○ Hoover Dam took years to build.

8. A ○ Don't tell my secret, please.
   B ○ Finally, she remembered his name.
   C ○ No amount of time will ease the pain.
   D ○ The nurse, a young man, saved her life.

Choose the correct verb(s) to complete each sentence.

9. I ____ waiting here for an hour. A ○ been B ○ had C ○ have been
10. Did Kurt tell you that these ____ his photographs? A ○ was B ○ is C ○ are
11. He ____ work at the library this year. A ○ don't B ○ doesn't C ○ doing
12. ____ I have your new phone number? A ○ May B ○ Does C ○ Can
13. Can you ____ me how to play the guitar? A ○ learn B ○ learned C ○ teach
14. Will Joan have time to ____ down before lunch? A ○ lie B ○ set C ○ lay
15. She ____ speak if there is time. A ○ may B ○ was C ○ is
16. Please ____ the book on the table. A ○ lie B ○ set C ○ sit
17. He said he ____ want any meat. A ○ don't B ○ doesn't C ○ do
18. It takes time to ____ something new. A ○ learn B ○ teach C ○ taught
19. ____ Carol going to pick up her package? A ○ Are B ○ Were C ○ Is
20. I am going to ____ down now. A ○ lie B ○ lay C ○ lying
21. She wants to ____ how to ski. A ○ teach B ○ learned C ○ learn
22. Jason ____ need anything from the store. A ○ do B ○ doesn't C ○ don't

Name ______________________________

Choose the correct past tense verb to complete each sentence.

23. Several of us ___ in a play. A ○ had sang B ○ sung C ○ have sung

24. I ___ my favorite vase yesterday. A ○ broke B ○ had broke C ○ broken

25. We ___ to the park for lunch. A ○ gone B ○ went C ○ have went

26. The bottle of soda ___ . A ○ freezed B ○ frozed C ○ froze

27. She ___ out her old clothes. A ○ throw B ○ thrown C ○ threw

28. Who ___ this story? A ○ wrote B ○ write C ○ written

29. Sylvia ___ her a present. A ○ gived B ○ gave C ○ given

Choose the correct adjective or adverb to complete each sentence.

30. This is the ___ ice cream I've ever had. A ○ smoother B ○ smoothest C ○ most smooth

31. A squirrel can run ___ than a dog. A ○ quickest B ○ quickly C ○ more quickly

Choose the correct pronoun to complete each sentence.

32. Have you ever met ___ parents? A ○ hers B ○ their C ○ them

33. ___ was waiting for me when I got home. A ○ They B ○ Both C ○ No one

34. ___ and Laurel are going to the concert tonight. A ○ He B ○ Him C ○ Her

35. Please tell ___ to meet us at six o'clock. A ○ them B ○ their C ○ they

36. Chuck gave the prettiest flower to ___ . A ○ she B ○ hers C ○ her

37. It was ___ who cooked the turkey. A ○ her B ○ we C ○ us

38. Nina chose ___ as her partner? A ○ whom B ○ she C ○ who

Choose the correct word to go with the article.

39. a A ○ house B ○ onion C ○ umbrella

40. an A ○ tornado B ○ boat C ○ icicle

Choose whether each underlined group of words is (A) a prepositional phrase used as an adjective, (B) a prepositional phrase used as an adverb, or (C) not a prepositional phrase.

41. I learned about outdoor safety at a seminar. A ○ B ○ C ○

42. We all liked our instructor from England. A ○ B ○ C ○

43. She was very knowledgeable about safety. A ○ B ○ C ○

 Name ______________________________

Choose the word in each sentence that should be capitalized.

1. I had sweet and sour chicken at a chinese restaurant.

   A ○ sweet B ○ chicken C ○ chinese D ○ restaurant

2. My parents celebrated their wedding anniversary in may.

   A ○ parents B ○ wedding C ○ anniversary D ○ may

3. Who wrote the adventure story *The Call of the wild*?

   A ○ wrote B ○ adventure C ○ story D ○ *wild*

4. I met mayor Bradley at the celebration yesterday.

   A ○ met B ○ mayor C ○ celebration D ○ yesterday

5. She lives at 503 north Bryer Street, on the corner near the store.

   A ○ corner B ○ store C ○ north D ○ near

6. The earthquake shook the ground in Los Angeles, california.

   A ○ california B ○ earthquake C ○ ground D ○ shook

Choose the correct answer to the question.

In which sentences are commas used correctly?

7. A ○ I called, but Amy wasn't home.
   B ○ We ate cheese, apples and bread.
   C ○ "No" she said "I, can't go."
   D ○ The answer is, that we just don't know.

8. A ○ Stop look, and listen Bob.
   B ○ "We would like to go," said Hans.
   C ○ Enrique, my friend lives, in Houston.
   D ○ My arm hurts but, it's okay.

9. A ○ My best friend, Pat and I can come.
   B ○ Tell me now, what you want.
   C ○ Well, yes, I do like spinach.
   D ○ I left and then, Karen went home.

10. A ○ Tanya, did you see the show?
    B ○ Becky asked "How are you, Eric?"
    C ○ Well, how will you get there Jay?
    D ○ She told the truth, and was not believed.

Choose the correct answer to the question.

In which sentences is end punctuation used correctly?

11. A ○ How wonderful our trip was?
    B ○ I can't remember.
    C ○ Are you going to the fair!
    D ○ I just love this book so much.

12. A ○ Wow. That's a great album.
    B ○ Can you go with us!
    C ○ Have you seen a shooting star?
    D ○ What a great ceremony?

13. A ○ Take control of the car.
    B ○ Please, will you come!
    C ○ Don't I know you.
    D ○ Let me read that first?

14. A ○ That program was awful?
    B ○ Could you hear her sing!
    C ○ Let me watch for them.
    D ○ Ouch. That hurt.

Name ______________________________

Choose the correct answers to each question.

In which sentences are quotation marks used correctly?

15. A ○ “No,” said Tom, “I can’t go.
 B ○ “Are you leaving?” asked Lee.
 C ○ “Yes, said Joe, I am.”
 D ○ Carol said, Be sure to write!”

16. A ○ “How are you”? asked Dan
 B ○ “How, asked Sue, do you do it?”
 C ○ “When can you come?” I asked.
 D ○ “Yes! said Marie, “I can.”

17. A ○ For now, I’ll just wait,” said Todd.
 B ○ “Why don’t you ask? said Luis.
 C ○ “Please let me in!” said Carmen.
 D ○ “No, said Jeff, “I’m not ready yet.”

18. A ○ Brent said, “Throw that away.”
 B ○ “It’s still good, said Rebecca.”
 C ○ “Now,” said Lily, just watch me!”
 D ○ “Don’t forget to jump, said Ruth.

In which sentences are apostrophes used correctly?

19. A ○ I ca’nt meet you until 6:30.
 B ○ Il’l walk the dog.
 C ○ It’s 12:00, and I am late!
 D ○ The dog shook it’s head.

20. A ○ I’m sorry I can’t be there.
 B ○ Lets’ go together.
 C ○ I need two day’s notice.
 D ○ Were all staying home.

21. A ○ Tell them the’yre almost here.
 B ○ Our neighbor’s party was loud.
 C ○ Two trees’ caught on fire.
 D ○ Listen to the’ir reasons.

22. A ○ The picture tell’s the story.
 B ○ I love Charlotte’s home.
 C ○ His cats’ were both black.
 D ○ The papers have’nt been delivered.

Choose the correct answers to each question.

In which sentences or phrases are colons used correctly?

23. A ○ Dear Mom:
 B ○ Sincerely yours:
 C ○ 10:30 P.M.
 D ○ 615 A.M.

24. A ○ Take these things: a book, a pen, and some paper.
 B ○ Leave the house by 1130, or you’ll be late.
 C ○ Don’t worry: I’m fine.
 D ○ She called the following: names.

25. A ○ Dear Sir:
 B ○ The play begins at 83:0.
 C ○ Please: use this door.
 D ○ Thank you: for all your help.

In which sentences are hyphens used correctly?

26. A ○ My father-in-law came to visit.
 B ○ My part time-job is fun.
 C ○ There were more than thirty two-people.
 D ○ One half-of the cake was eaten.

27. A ○ Dorothy was fif-teen minutes late.
 B ○ A firefighter gave a presenta-tion on fire safety.
 C ○ Twenty six-pizzas were delivered to the party.
 D ○ That monument is over one-hundred years old.

28. A ○ The air conditioner was-broken.
 B ○ She is twenty-one years old.
 C ○ The sun-set was orange red.
 D ○ He likes his sister in-law.

 Name ____________________

Read the paragraph. Then choose the correct answer to each question.

Did you know that penguins actually prefer to live in very cold climates? In fact, most often they lay their eggs on ice. Fortunately, a penguin has thick layers of fat to help keep it warm. Some male penguins actually have extra rolls of fat, which they use to keep their newborn penguins warm. Originally, penguins were capable of flying, but millions of years ago, their wings developed into flippers which now function as paddles. Perhaps the most interesting thing of all about a penguin is the way it walks. Penguins actually waddle because they have such extremely short legs!

1. Which sentence can best be used as a topic sentence for the paragraph above?

A ○ Penguins like cold weather.

B ○ Male penguins care for their young.

C ○ The penguin is an unusual bird.

D ○ Penguins lay eggs.

2. Which sentence would be the best supporting detail for the paragraph above?

A ○ Penguins live in the southern half of the world.

B ○ Penguins are popular additions to most zoos.

C ○ All penguins are black and white.

D ○ The male penguin produces a milky substance in its throat, which it uses to feed its young.

3. Which audience would be the most interested in this paragraph?

A ○ grandparents **B** ○ soccer coaches **C** ○ animal lovers **D** ○ nurses

Choose the sentence that does not contain details that support the topic sentence.

4. Topic Sentence: A chef's job is very demanding.

A ○ Great chefs can make very good money.

B ○ Chefs must cook many things at once.

C ○ They must make sure a party's meals are ready at the same time.

D ○ Chefs must cook food as quickly as possible.

5. Topic Sentence: Wild mustangs are increasing in number.

A ○ People with ranches are letting mustangs roam free.

B ○ Wild mustangs are smaller than other breeds.

C ○ Some people adopt wild mustangs and care for them.

D ○ The government is protecting more land for mustangs to use.

Name ____________________

Choose the correct answer to each question.

6. Which is not good advice for taking research notes?
   - A ○ Use reference materials for information.
   - B ○ Take notes, then organize research questions.
   - C ○ Always put information in your own words.
   - D ○ Take more notes than you expect to need.

7. Which is not part of an outline?
   - A ○ subheadings
   - B ○ title
   - C ○ main headings
   - D ○ topic sentence

8. Which is not part of a report?
   - A ○ title
   - B ○ main headings
   - C ○ topic sentences
   - D ○ informative paragraphs

9. Which is not part of a business letter?
   - A ○ body
   - B ○ heading
   - C ○ signature
   - D ○ title

10. Which is not part of writing a good business letter?
    - A ○ Reread and rewrite, if necessary.
    - B ○ Use the person's first name in the greeting.
    - C ○ Include specific information.
    - D ○ Use business-size paper and envelopes.

11. Which part of a business letter follows the body?
    - A ○ greeting
    - B ○ heading
    - C ○ inside address
    - D ○ closing

Choose the correct revision of each underlined sentence.

12. <u>dr. Jones came I and Paul visited with him</u>
    - A ○ When Dr. Jones came Paul and I visited with him.
    - B ○ When Mr. Jones visited, I and Paul came with him.
    - C ○ Dr. Jones came, and Paul and I visited with him.
    - D ○ When Dr. Jones came, Paul and I visited with him.

13. <u>tell Kay what that she herd was a the secret</u>
    - A ○ Tell Kay, what she herd was the secret.
    - B ○ Tell Kay what she heard that was a secret.
    - C ○ Tell Kay that what she heard was a secret.
    - D ○ Tell Kay there what she heard.

14. <u>the gold rush, people streamed form over all the country to Californa</u>
    - A ○ All the people from the country streamed to California.
    - B ○ During the Gold Rush, people from all over went to California.
    - C ○ People streamed from all over the country to the Gold Rush.
    - D ○ During the Gold Rush, people from all over the country streamed to California.

 Name ______________________

Refer to the dictionary samples to answer the questions that follow.

leav-en (lev′en) *n.* **1.** a substance that causes dough to rise. **2.** a small piece of such dough put aside to be used for causing other dough to rise. *-v.* to cause dough to rise. [Middle English, from Old French, from Latin *levein.*]
left (left) *adj.* toward the side of the body that is westward when facing north. *-n.* that which is on the left. *-adv.* toward the left. [Middle English lift, from Old English *lyft,* weak.]
let (let) *v.* **1.** to permit or allow: *Did he let you go?* **2.** to allow to pass through: *I let the bird out of its cage.* **3.** to make; cause: *They'll let us know.* **4.** to rent. [Old English *laeten,* to allow.]

1. Which word has two syllables?
A ○ leaven **B** ○ left **C** ○ let

2. Which is the pronunciation of leaven?
A ○ (lyft) **B** ○ (laeten) **C** ○ (lev′en)

3. Which word has the most definitions?
A ○ leaven **B** ○ let **C** ○ left

4. As which part of speech can left not be used?
A ○ pronoun **B** ○ adjective **C** ○ adverb

5. Which word originally meant "weak"?
A ○ let **B** ○ left **C** ○ leaven

6. From how many other languages did leaven come?
A ○ two **B** ○ three **C** ○ four

Choose the correct answer to each question.

7. Where would you find the publisher of a book? **A** ○ title page **B** ○ index **C** ○ copyright page

8. Where would you find chapter titles? **A** ○ table of contents **B** ○ index **C** ○ title page

Tell which kind of catalog card you would refer to in order to find the book(s). Choose (A) for author card, (B) for subject card, or (C) for title card.

9. books about volcanoes in Hawaii **A** ○ **B** ○ **C** ○

10. *To Kill a Mockingbird* **A** ○ **B** ○ **C** ○

11. a book of short stories by O. Henry **A** ○ **B** ○ **C** ○

12. books about Grandma Moses **A** ○ **B** ○ **C** ○

13. a book of poems by Carl Sandburg **A** ○ **B** ○ **C** ○

14. *The Story of Martin Luther King* **A** ○ **B** ○ **C** ○

Tell which reference you would use to find the following information. Choose (A) for dictionary, (B) for encyclopedia, (C) for atlas, or (D) for thesaurus.

15. the distance from Kansas City to Chicago **A** ○ **B** ○ **C** ○ **D** ○

16. information about mural painting **A** ○ **B** ○ **C** ○ **D** ○

17. the etymology of the word define **A** ○ **B** ○ **C** ○ **D** ○

18. the history of doll collecting **A** ○ **B** ○ **C** ○ **D** ○

19. an antonym for the word increase **A** ○ **B** ○ **C** ○ **D** ○

20. the pronunciation of the word technology **A** ○ **B** ○ **C** ○ **D** ○

Name ______________________

Use the chart and the graph to answer the questions.

Soda Sales Chart

Day	Cases of Grape	Cases of Cherry
Monday	10	6
Tuesday	4	20
Wednesday	8	16
Thursday	12	6
Friday	14	10

Soda Sales Graph

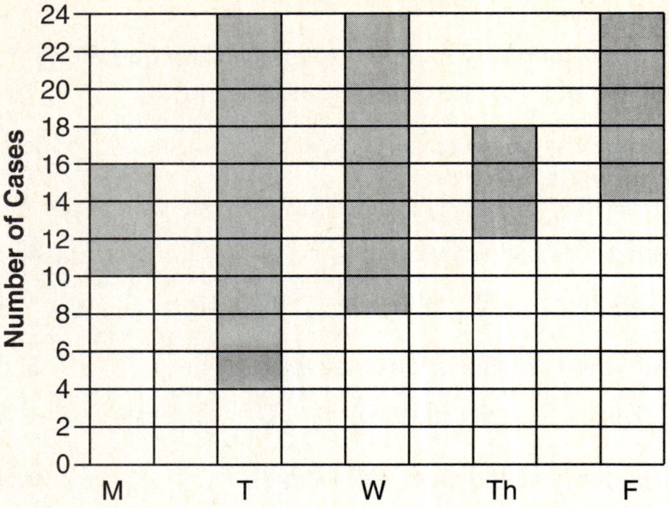

Graph Key	
Grape	☐
Cherry	■

21. On which day was the most grape soda sold?

A ○ Monday C ○ Thursday

B ○ Wednesday D ○ Friday

22. On which days was the same amount of cherry soda sold?

A ○ Monday and Wednesday

B ○ Tuesday and Friday

C ○ Monday and Thursday

D ○ Thursday and Friday

23. On which day was twice as much cherry soda sold as grape?

A ○ Tuesday C ○ Thursday

B ○ Wednesday D ○ Friday

Use the map to answer the questions.

Center Zoo

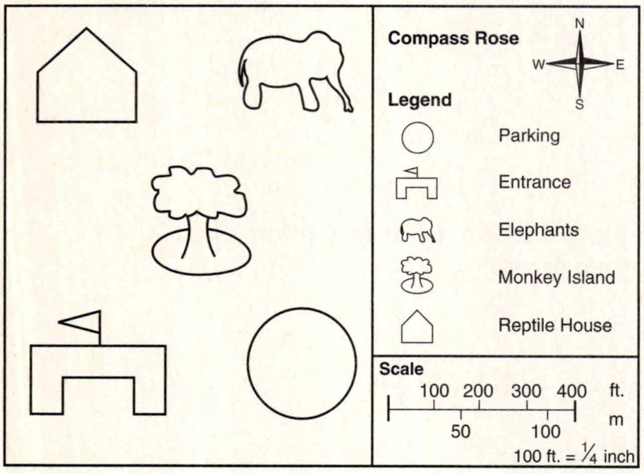

24. Which direction is the entrance from the parking area?

A ○ north C ○ east

B ○ south D ○ west

25. Which direction would you go to get to the reptile house from the entrance?

A ○ north C ○ east

B ○ south D ○ west

26. Which direction would you walk to get to your car after seeing the elephants?

A ○ north C ○ east

B ○ south D ○ west

27. About how far is it from the center of the parking area to Monkey Island?

A ○ about 100 feet, or 30 meters

B ○ about 200 feet, or 61 meters

C ○ about 300 feet, or 91 meters

D ○ about 400 feet, or 122 meters

 Name ______________________